Stephen Burman is Dean of Humanities at the University of Sussex, UK. His books include *America in the Modern World: The Transcendence of US Hegemony* and *The Black Progress Question: Explaining the African-American Predicament*, which received a Gustavus Myers Award for outstanding work in the field of human rights.

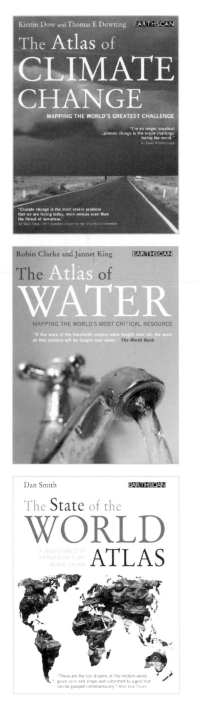

THE ~~ ~~ THE
AMERICAN EMPIRE

First published by Earthscan in the UK in 2007

A catalogue record for this book is available from the British Library

ISBN: 978-1-84407-428-0

Produced for Earthscan by
Myriad Editions
59 Lansdowne Place
Brighton, BN3 1FL, UK
www.MyriadEditions.com

Edited and co-ordinated by Jannet King and Candida Lacey
Maps and graphics created by Isabelle Lewis
Design and additional graphics by Corinne Pearlman

Printed on paper produced from sustainable sources.
Printed and bound in Hong Kong through Phoenix Offset
under the supervision of Bob Cassels, The Hanway Press, London

For a full list of publications please contact:

Earthscan
8–12 Camden High Street
London, NW1 0JH, UK
Tel: +44 (0)20 7387 8558
Fax: +44 (0)20 7387 8998
Email: earthinfo@earthscan.co.uk
Web: www.earthscan.co.uk

Earthscan publishes in association with
the International Institute for Environment and Development

This one is for George

CONTENTS

Chapter Four: PEOPLE

Immigration
There has been a dramatic change in the pattern of immigration to the USA since 1965.

The Americas
US domination of its hemisphere is being transformed by mass migration of Latin Americans into the USA.

Economic Migration
More people are living outside their country of birth than ever before, leading to a tighter integration of rich and poor countries.

Political Refugees
American influence in political upheaval and conflicts has contributed to the displacement of millions of people.

Chapter Five: MILITARY

Military Spending
US military spending has fluctuated in response to perceived threats and presidential ambitions for world domination.

Comparative Military Spending
US military spending is greater than that of the next five largest spenders combined, giving the USA a military might beyond that of any other state.

Military at Home
Military spending boosts local economies. Defense spending, and thus foreign policy, is therefore partly driven by domestic political pressures.

Military Abroad
US overseas bases and military personnel symbolize the power that defines American imperialism.

Arms Sales
The USA is the world's largest arms exporter, and the US government manipulates this trade to influence world events.

Chapter Six: SECURITY

Interventions: 1945–89
During the Cold War, the USA intervened in over 30 countries to prevent the spread of communism.

Interventions: 1990–2006
Since the end of the Cold War, the USA has relied increasingly on military intervention to implement its foreign policy.

Interventions: Military and Covert
Although the USA never sees itself as an aggressor, it has a long record of intervening in the internal affairs of other countries to protect its interests.

The Pacific Rim
With many of the world's leading powers emerging in the region, the Pacific Rim is likely to become the main focus of US foreign policy.

Europe, Middle East and Africa
Although the threat to US security from the ex-Soviet Union has disappeared, new threats have emerged from the Middle East.

ACKNOWLEDGMENTS

All books are collaborations, but some are more collaborative than others. This book is truly a team effort and could not have been created by the named author alone. The other members of the team, to all of whom I am indebted, are:

Michèle Harrison who, in addition to being a sounding board for many of the ideas in this book, assisted with the research in the midst of many other duties, mastering the intricacies of data in fields new to her and always finding information that provoked thought.

Sadie Mayne, the first editor for this project, who moved on to nurturing in a much more significant capacity. Jannet King picked up the mantle, and her scrupulousness in checking data, and bringing order to its presentation, has been indefatigable. More importantly, nothing illogical or merely casual in argument or expression survived her forensic inspection, and such rigor as this book possesses is due in no small part to her contribution.

Isabelle Lewis, whose creative talent in transforming, without fuss or fury, mere words and facts into dynamic visual imagery has made a major impact on this book and has also made her a joy to work with.

Corinne Pearlman, who combines design skills with an acute political intelligence that keeps an author on his toes.

Leading and inspiring all of the talent at Myriad Editions is Candida Lacey, whose professional skills I had heard much about. Having now benefited from them myself, I know that her reputation for creativity and imagination, combined with drive and practicality, is amply justified.

To demonstrate just how much the Myriad team contributed to this book I am tempted to disclaim the usual disclaimer and offer to share any blame for mistakes, but that would be wrong and I take full responsibility for any errors.

Writing a book is a personal as well as a professional activity and incurs debts accordingly. Few books fail to consume their authors in both respects at some point and this is no exception. When that line is blurred, families bear the brunt and partners most of all. I am especially grateful to Candida for that reason. Children, too, are called on to make sacrifices in which they had no choosing. Ours, Eve and George, have been brilliant, tolerant and supportive in this venture as in everything else. Eve has had her turn and, as all the family knows, this one, with love and respect, is for George.

Stephen Burman
April 2007

Introduction

AN IMPERIAL HISTORY?

The USA is the only nation whose influence is truly global. The demise of the Soviet Union at the beginning of the 1990s left it without a military rival and, in the 21st century, its international role has been described increasingly in terms of empire. This is not intended to imply the territorial conquest and direct rule characteristic of past empires, such as those of the Romans, Ottomans, and British, but is a useful construct within which to consider America's multifarious role in shaping the contemporary world.

Many Americans may be reluctant to consider their country as an imperial nation. In the Declaration of Independence of 1776, the Founding Fathers declared, as the first principle of their philosophy of government, "We hold these truths to be self-evident, that all men are created equal" – a sentiment not compatible with an imperial mentality. Throughout its history, the USA has not generally sought or retained colonies, even when its power has permitted it to do so. In the aftermath of the First World War, President Woodrow Wilson used American influence to dismantle European empires and to create a just peace on the principle of self-determination. Later, in 1941, President Franklin D. Roosevelt, in a speech on the day before Pearl Harbor, looked to create a world based on four essential human freedoms: freedom of speech, freedom of worship, freedom from want, and freedom from fear. These principles came to underpin the UN Declaration on Human Rights in 1948, which many would argue has guided US foreign policy since the Second World War.

There is another perspective on American history, however, which paints a different picture. The settlement of North America by Europeans can be seen as an invasion of land that belonged to native inhabitants, and US treatment of native Americans in the century or more after independence bore all the hallmarks of what today we call ethnic cleansing. Fifteen percent of the total area of the USA is land that was purchased under duress from Mexico as a condition of the end of the Mexican–American War of 1846–48. In foreign policy, too, the USA showed empire-building tendencies. In 1823, President James Monroe formulated a doctrine that the USA would act to prevent European powers interfering in the affairs of the Americas. At the beginning of the 20th century, in 1904, President Theodore Roosevelt extended the Monroe Doctrine to assert the right of the USA to intervene in the

> " THE UNITED STATES IS UNIQUE BECAUSE WE ARE AN EMPIRE OF IDEALS. "
>
> RONALD REAGAN
> US PRESIDENT
> 1980–88

affairs of Latin American nations, and to exercise an international police power. In the 20th century there have been 180 instances of the use of US armed forces abroad in situations of military conflict or potential conflict, or for other than normal peacetime purposes.

Although America has moved a long way from the Founding Fathers' original intentions, its foreign policy has always had a mixture of motives, from idealism to economic self-interest, and a range of modes, from isolationism to intervention. This combination has rarely involved the significant territorial control or direct administration of other societies that was exercised by earlier empires. The USA has not generally sought long-term relationships with those it has disempowered, which is the way to ensure steady imperial rule; rather, its engagement with other societies tends to be transient, goal-oriented, and too specific for the long-term control implied by classic imperialism.

What the USA does have in common with, for example, the empires of the Romans (31 BCE–CE 476), the Ottomans (c.1281–1922) and the British (1583–1971), however, is the ability to affect outcomes and make other societies do their bidding. If we accept that empire is not just about direct control of governments or territory, but about dominating global trade and capital flows, exerting political and economic influence, maintaining worldwide military domination, and spawning a homogenized global culture, then America can be seen as having become an imperial nation. Empire is only ever a metaphor for America's role in the contemporary world, but the profile of US power makes it an appropriate one.

GLOBALIZATION AND EMPIRE

US power has undoubtedly grown in recent years. It is the only superpower in the age of globalization, and some argue that it has become the most powerful nation in history because of its unprecedented global reach. But globalization, which is the increased movement of people, goods, and capital across national boundaries, raises the question of whether all nation states, including the USA, have been replaced as the driving force in international affairs by a single, interconnected world system. And if the nation state has become redundant, then talking about American imperialism becomes pointless. The difficulty with this argument, however, is that a world system does not run itself. There have to be rules for the conduct of economic and political activities, and the power to enforce them. In inter-state relations, there is little equivalent to domestic law for maintaining order, and, in the absence of a single, global governing authority, nation states are the only form of organization that can resolve conflicts of interest because only they have the authority and resources to enforce agreements. This is as true when dealing with new transnational threats, such as terrorism and environmental degradation, as it is of traditional inter-state rivalries.

But if nation states remain a vital force, what is to prevent them pursuing their interests in security and prosperity in such a way that leads to a war of all against all? Who will formulate and enforce the rules that co-ordinate interests and impose discipline so as to avoid the danger of chaos in international affairs and steer the international system towards a productive response to the challenges that face it?

There are several possible configurations of power that can achieve this. At one end of the spectrum is a world in which there is consensus on the principles of government and in which all states abide by the rules voluntarily. Less idealistically, states co-operate not because they agree, but because there is a balance of power between them. A more realistic configuration is one in which there is an imbalance of power between states, but in which the dominant state or states take responsibility for keeping order. The dominant state can use its power in either a benign or a selfish manner. The term *hegemony* describes a system in which leadership is exercised on behalf of all, there is a consensus of values, authority is legitimate, and there is security and prosperity for both the ruled and the rulers. *Imperialism* is the more appropriate term for when a dominant state acts only for its own interests, there is no consensus, authority is not legitimate, order is achieved through force, and benefits are confined to the rulers. All international systems operate by a mixture of force and consent and today's is no different. As the world's dominant power, America presides over a global system between these two extremes, and its role contains elements of both hegemony and imperialism.

In earlier eras, empires were based on conquest and colonization, supported by military power and control of territory. Today, the world system is characterized by relatively free markets in which the primary resource is capital. To work effectively, the market system, which is based on the free movement of capital, goods and people, requires co-operation and stability. The USA is central to the development of a new global regime of international power, but it has to work within the constraints imposed by the interdependence inherent in globalization. This precludes the USA from exercising the cruder forms of imperial power. As the world's leading power it has an indispensable role in creating a framework for co-operation rather than in furthering its own narrow interests. This imperative drives the USA towards a role in which it is more than a leader but less than an empire, and where power is exercised indirectly rather than by America imposing its will on other societies.

THE AMERICAN PROFILE

America's role in the world is not governed solely by the requirements of the world system. It also has a unique profile of strengths and weaknesses that affect its policies. Among its strengths is its immense economic power. The American economy has been the driving force of the world economy, and its position until recently was reinforced by the dominant role of the US dollar in world finance and by its strong influence over the international financial institutions that have direct responsibility for global prosperity. And yet, despite its great wealth, the USA is now also the world's largest debtor nation. It runs trade deficits that make it dependent on investment by surplus nations and on their continued co-operation. The USA is also vulnerable because it is increasingly dependent on overseas sources for energy supplies; making these more secure is an important driver of its foreign policy.

The area of greatest US pre-eminence is undoubtedly the military, where its spending and firepower dwarf that of any other nation. Strength in this area is vital to the maintenance of any empire, and its national security strategy commits the USA to maintaining an unchallengeable military position. However, the possession of overwhelming military power is not a sufficient condition for successful imperial rule because it cannot overcome the inherent limitation of military force, namely that its use creates resistance and resentment among those defeated. Military force can be an effective short-term means of defense or conquest, but it is not a basis for long-term rule or a stable international order. Long-term rule requires some degree of consent from the ruled and in order to command consent qualities that lie in the realm of ideas are needed. The USA enjoys a dominant place in global consumer culture as a counterpart to its economic strength, but the higher ideals on which America was founded also command widespread assent and respect across the world. By representing these ideals, the USA has enjoyed an exemplary status that is another source of strength critical to its capacity to rule.

An important part of America's profile is the self image of its people, and here, too, the picture is mixed. A strong diffidence towards exercising world leadership is a continuing element in American political culture. And yet one key characteristic of empire is the belief of a people in its own superiority as a basis for the will to rule, and this is not lacking in the American psyche. During the period of westward expansion until the frontier was closed at the end of the 19th century, the occupation of land was an important aspect of American identity but, over the sweep of the 20th century, America, unlike many of its European forbears, has found its identity in its ideals, its people, and its dominance of world trade rather than in territory. Its self image is that of an exemplary society, whose genius lies in the balance between individual freedom and opportunity in the public sphere, and between ethnic diversity, community, and support at the private level. This balance has permitted the USA to face, far better than most countries, the challenges of immigration and multiculturalism that are becoming increasingly important in the 21st century. The consequence is a mentality in which American superiority towards other peoples is expressed in terms of emulation rather than conquest – an attitude enhanced by America's relative geographic isolation, and by the sense of inviolability and immunity from invasion it has traditionally enjoyed.

US POLICIES AFTER 9/11

This sense of inviolability was of course shattered by 9/11, which threatened America's sense of security as perhaps nothing else since Pearl Harbor in 1941. The result is to reinforce many Americans' belief in the superiority of their culture rather than to undermine it. The idea of US territory as a homeland that has to be protected has taken root. America has developed a stronger sense of its borders, becoming a less open and welcoming society. It is more suspicious of other cultures, and a strong domestic tradition of civil liberty is threatened in the name of protecting national security. The damage that 9/11 has done to the American psyche has led to a relatively aggressive response, since defense of the homeland cannot stop at the borders and must be pursued wherever those responsible for the atrocity are to be found. Although the USA disavows imperial ambition, in Washington the imperial mentality has become prevalent since 9/11, and many see America's government as evolving, like that of Ancient Rome, from a genuine republic to a presidency that is imperial in all but name. This stance has led much of the rest of the world to reject the idea of America as a freedom-loving democracy. Indeed, the opposite view has gained ground and, since 9/11, much of the world now sees America not as an example, whose values and institutions command admiration and have universal relevance, but as the incarnation of imperialism, intent on imposing its own values and trampling on the rights of others in the name of self-defense.

The tendencies responsible for this perception were evident before 9/11. During the Cold War, the USA created a relatively stable world order that commanded support in many parts of the world. But even at the height of the triumph over communism, when the Soviet Union collapsed in 1991 after a decade of assertive projection of American power under President Reagan, the USA was concerned that the burdens of empire were too great. Facing a new set of challenges, in what had become a globalized world, America initially lacked a sense of how to maintain its leadership. Exceptional economic growth in the 1990s allowed the USA to take the initiative in shaping the rules for a new world economic order, most notably through the creation of the World Trade Organization. As America projected its own free-market system on to the new world economy, continuing economic growth in the late 1990s restored confidence, not only in the market system, but also in the wider conception of democracy and human rights that Americans see as the other pillar of a free society. This led to a more ambitious agenda to spread the American ideas across the world. Efforts to promote this agenda did not always meet with immediate success – effective intervention in the Balkans being counterbalanced by failure to produce peace in Palestine – but by the end of the 20th century the USA had secured its pre-eminent role in the world system and turned the challenge of globalization into a source of strength.

In the 21st century, American policy has become even more expansive. The Bush administration has taken its agenda to new heights, seeking to remake the world in the image of its ideals of freedom and democracy. The idealism of the Bush administration has been tempered by hard-headed realism, but it has been consistently driven by a religiously inspired vision of America's duty and right to spread its values across the world. This has been accompanied by a belief in its capacity to change the world, based on the possession of a uniquely strong set of assets: military might, a large and booming economy, nuclear dominance, territorial immunity from attack, and the power of its ideals. The aftermath of the war in Iraq demonstrates that the Bush administration has overestimated its capacity to effect change. The principal arena for this has been the Middle East, where grandiose US ambitions to impose democratization have been exposed as a folly and where, even worse, America's demonizing of Islam has proven a self-fulfilling prophecy by alienating and radicalizing large swathes of the Muslim world.

The aggression associated with these policies is encapsulated in the Bush doctrine for the conduct of US foreign policy, which has replaced deterrence and containment with military superiority, pre-emptive action in the face of potential threat, unilateralism, and a commitment to export American-style democracy across the globe. American assertiveness is also driven by fear in the face of a new set of threats crystallized by 9/11. US policy in the 21st century has undergone a qualitative shift from the assertive multilateralism of the late Clinton years to an engaged unilateralism under Bush, extending even to a temporary territorial imperialism in Iraq and Afghanistan. It is this change of policy, and the actions that have accompanied it, which, when combined with objective US strength in economic, military, political, and cultural terms, have given rise to talk of empire. 9/11 is not the reason for this shift, but it is the catalyst that was needed to make Bush's grand strategy come alive. That strategy has proven flawed because the USA has over-reached the limits of its power and is suffering blowback as a result of moving down the road from hegemony to empire.

THE FUTURE OF THE AMERICAN EMPIRE
As a result of America's hubristic approach to foreign policy in the 21st century, and the discredit the USA is suffering as a consequence, we have passed the high watermark of American imperialism. The next phase in US policy, which may have to wait until President George W. Bush's successor takes office, is likely to see a reversion to a less aggressive and more multilateral approach. Making this change will be difficult because American prestige has been engaged in an unsuccessful venture in Iraq, and failure has damaged its credibility as a superpower on the wider international stage. The USA needs to find a way to extricate itself from the debacle in the Middle East before it can move on to reassert its power on a more sustainable basis.

America will continue to employ idealist rhetoric in support of its policies, but will re-learn how to combine this with greater pragmatism in practice. It will seek to manage the world system less directly, making tactical withdrawals from hotspots, while continuing to manipulate the balance of power in regions of potential conflict. It will become more even-handed and resume the role of honest broker in areas of conflict such as the Middle East, and in Asia. Its approach will be less censorious and more tolerant of diverse systems, and will avoid setting preconditions for talks or requiring others to follow its agenda. America will only be successful if it re-establishes a consensual approach to world governance as its pattern of rule, relying more on the power of its ideas to win hearts and minds, and abandoning the attempt to impose its ways and its will on others in what has proven to be a ruinous imperial detour from the long trajectory of American power.

No empire lasts forever and, if we speculate as to what may happen in the longer term, trends suggest that, after a long period in which American power has grown almost uninterruptedly, the USA will decline from its current pinnacle. The most obvious challenge is the rise of China, whose combination of a market economy and political authoritarianism may create a Beijing consensus to replace the Washington consensus that has been the hallmark of the first phase of globalization. But China's rise is likely to be only part of a more general shift of power to Asia. The first phase of globalization has been strongly associated with the Americanization of the world, but the shift to Asia in economic and eventually political, maybe even military, terms means that by 2050 globalization is more likely to be associated with Asianization – a fact on which the USA seems insufficiently focused, preoccupied as it is with the Middle East and with its War on Terror.

In this context, the major challenge facing the USA is to manage its own relative decline and effect a transition from its uniquely powerful position in the early 21st century to a position where it is one power in a multi-polar world. It is unlikely voluntarily to hand over the keys of empire as smoothly as the British did to their American cousins in the middle of the 20th century, but trying to maintain its pre-eminence beyond its natural life will only put the USA at odds with the rising forces in world politics. The USA will retain the military capacity to resist challenges to its power, but reliance on force to preserve its position will escalate conflict to a level that would damage the stability of the world order and threaten a descent into barbarism. Managing a shift to a multi-polar world is a great test of American diplomacy, and it is a challenge it cannot meet alone. It will require co-operation from other states that is not assured, given the extent of inequality and insecurity globalization has brought to large parts of the world, and the anger, frustration, and radicalism this has generated. As the leading power, the USA must manage costs and benefits to its clients and its enemies so as to create a framework in which accommodation becomes the norm. If it succeeds, the USA will reconcile its national interest with global responsibility by providing benefits to others, as well as to itself. This may restore to America the status of "exemplary society" that it has so grievously lost through its ruinous imperial detour, and make the judgment of history on the USA more benign than now seems likely to all those currently suffering under its imperial yoke.

AMERICA'S GLOBAL FOOTPRINT

America makes its mark across the world, through
military strength, economic power, and the force of its
ideas and culture, to an extent unmatched by any
other country.

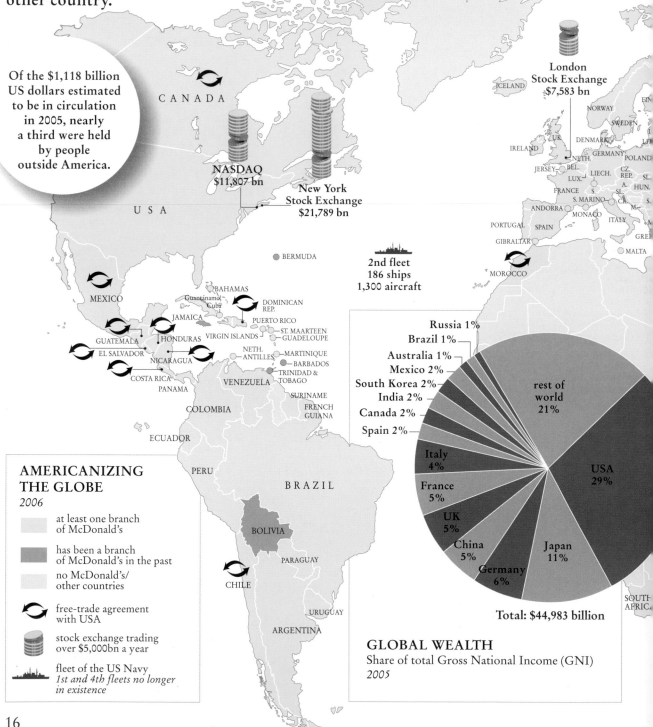

Of the $1,118 billion
US dollars estimated
to be in circulation
in 2005, nearly
a third were held
by people
outside America.

CANADA

London
Stock Exchange
$7,583 bn

ICELAND

NORWAY

SWEDEN

IRELAND   UK   DENMARK

JERSEY   NETH.   GERMANY   POLAND

LUX.   BEL.   LIECH.   CZ.
REP.

FRANCE   A.   HUN.

S.   SL.

ANDORRA   MONACO   S. MARINO   ITALY   GRE

PORTUGAL   SPAIN

GIBRALTAR   MALTA

MOROCCO

NASDAQ
$11,807 bn

New York
Stock Exchange
$21,789 bn

USA

BERMUDA

MEXICO

BAHAMAS
Guantánamo
Cuba

DOMINICAN
REP.

JAMAICA   PUERTO RICO

GUATEMALA   HONDURAS   VIRGIN ISLANDS   ST. MAARTEEN
GUADELOUPE

EL SALVADOR   NICARAGUA   NETH.
ANTILLES   MARTINIQUE

COSTA RICA   BARBADOS

PANAMA   VENEZUELA   TRINIDAD &
TOBAGO

SURINAME

COLOMBIA   FRENCH
GUIANA

ECUADOR

PERU   BRAZIL

2nd fleet
186 ships
1,300 aircraft

GLOBAL WEALTH
Share of total Gross National Income (GNI)
2005

Russia 1%
Brazil 1%
Australia 1%
Mexico 2%
South Korea 2%
India 2%
Canada 2%
Spain 2%

rest of
world
21%

Italy
4%

France
5%

UK
5%

China
5%

Germany
6%

USA
29%

Japan
11%

SOUTH
AFRIC

Total: $44,983 billion

AMERICANIZING THE GLOBE
2006

- at least one branch
  of McDonald's
- has been a branch
  of McDonald's in the past
- no McDonald's/
  other countries

↻ free-trade agreement
  with USA

stock exchange trading
over $5,000bn a year

fleet of the US Navy
*1st and 4th fleets no longer
in existence*

BOLIVIA

PARAGUAY

CHILE

URUGUAY

ARGENTINA

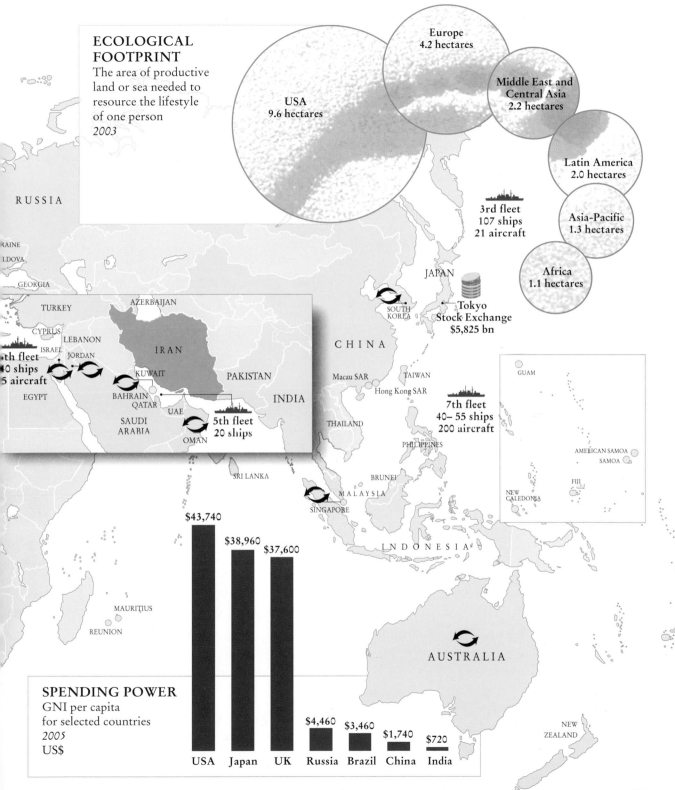

ECOLOGICAL FOOTPRINT

The area of productive land or sea needed to resource the lifestyle of one person
2003

USA
9.6 hectares

Europe
4.2 hectares

Middle East and Central Asia
2.2 hectares

Latin America
2.0 hectares

Asia-Pacific
1.3 hectares

Africa
1.1 hectares

3rd fleet
107 ships
21 aircraft

RUSSIA

GEORGIA

TURKEY

CYPRUS
LEBANON
ISRAEL
JORDAN
AZERBAIJAN

IRAN

KUWAIT
BAHRAIN
QATAR
UAE
SAUDI ARABIA
OMAN

EGYPT

PAKISTAN

INDIA

5th fleet
20 ships

th fleet
0 ships
5 aircraft

JAPAN

SOUTH KOREA

Tokyo Stock Exchange
$5,825 bn

CHINA

Macau SAR

TAIWAN

Hong Kong SAR

THAILAND

PHILIPPINES

BRUNEI

MALAYSIA
SINGAPORE

SRI LANKA

7th fleet
40– 55 ships
200 aircraft

GUAM

NEW CALEDONIA

AMERICAN SAMOA
SAMOA

FIJI

INDONESIA

MAURITIUS

REUNION

AUSTRALIA

NEW ZEALAND

$43,740

$38,960

$37,600

$4,460

$3,460

$1,740

$720

SPENDING POWER

GNI per capita for selected countries
2005
US$

USA	Japan	UK	Russia	Brazil	China	India

Chapter One

ENERGY

The rate at which we consume natural resources is putting the survival of the planet at risk. Few countries are self-sufficient, and competition is accelerating for the control of access to raw materials. Water, for example, is widely predicted to become the major motive for armed conflict in the 21st century. Even more alarming is the growth of global energy consumption, which, if it continues at present rates, will change the climate in ways that endanger the very survival of humanity. America's role is critical because it is by far the largest consumer of energy in the world.

The USA is not self-sufficient in raw materials, which it must import to feed its giant economy and military machine. Its national security is therefore dependent on maintaining access to commodities it cannot produce itself, of which energy is the most vital. US foreign policy is, in turn, driven by economic imperatives, even at the risk of conflict with other countries. In the opinion of many people, the real reason for the US intervention in Iraq in 2003 was not the stated rationale of promoting democracy and self-determination, upholding human rights and protecting citizens from terror, but to protect its access to supplies of oil.

Although the need for self-sufficiency in energy is growing in the USA, under the administration of George W. Bush a policy of securing stable energy supplies from abroad to protect the American standard of living takes precedence over concern for the environment. Its pro-growth stance drives classic imperialist behavior. This does not involve annexing territory, but requires intervention in the politics of other countries to ensure they make their supplies available to the international market. This is why the issue of energy has such a widespread effect on the USA's global political strategy.

> " THE GOOD LORD DIDN'T SEE FIT TO PUT OIL AND GAS ONLY WHERE THERE ARE DEMOCRATIC REGIMES FRIENDLY TO THE UNITED STATES. "
>
> DICK CHENEY
> CEO HALLIBURTON
> JUNE 1998

ENERGY CONSUMPTION

In order to support their lifestyle, Americans use five times the global average energy consumption.

The USA is not the largest consumer of energy per person – some countries with very cold weather or very cheap energy supplies consume up to three times US levels – but its history and culture of consumption have generated a profligate attitude to energy. Europe's energy use per person is just 40 percent of the USA's, despite its similar temperature range and level of economic development.

Transport use is a major factor in US energy production. The price of gasoline remains relatively low in the USA, enabling Americans to maintain their infatuation with the automobile and, more recently, an addiction to air travel. The consequence is that the USA produces 35 percent of the world's transport emissions of carbon dioxide.

The USA's high energy consumption is unsustainable. This is not only because of the impact it has on the global environment through global warming, it is not even because of the finite nature of the energy supply, though both are vitally important. The real issue is political. Supplies of energy simply do not exist to enable every country to raise

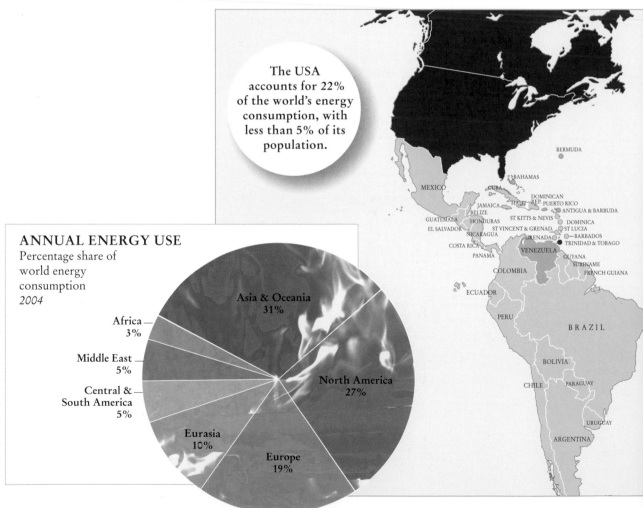

The USA accounts for 22% of the world's energy consumption, with less than 5% of its population.

ANNUAL ENERGY USE
Percentage share of world energy consumption
2004

Asia & Oceania 31%

Africa 3%

Middle East 5%

Central & South America 5%

Eurasia 10%

Europe 19%

North America 27%

its consumption to anything like the level of the USA, and the environmental impact would be catastrophic if they tried. And yet, quite naturally, others see no reason why Americans should have an exclusive right to a standard of living based on energy consumption that is denied to them.

The current situation is increasingly affecting US relations with the rest of the world and will lead to fundamental foreign policy choices. Either the USA will have to reduce its energy consumption to sustainable levels, of which there is as yet little sign, or it will have to protect its privileged position, at the expense of global equality. The latter will bring America into conflict with the rest of the world, in particular with increasingly powerful countries such as India and China. This conflict will extend beyond energy policy into trade and economic relations and, ultimately, has more potential to lead to military conflict than any other issue, as the wars in Iraq have so graphically demonstrated.

ENERGY USE
per person
2004
million Btu

- 300 or more
- 200 – 299
- 100 – 199
- 10 – 99
- fewer than 10

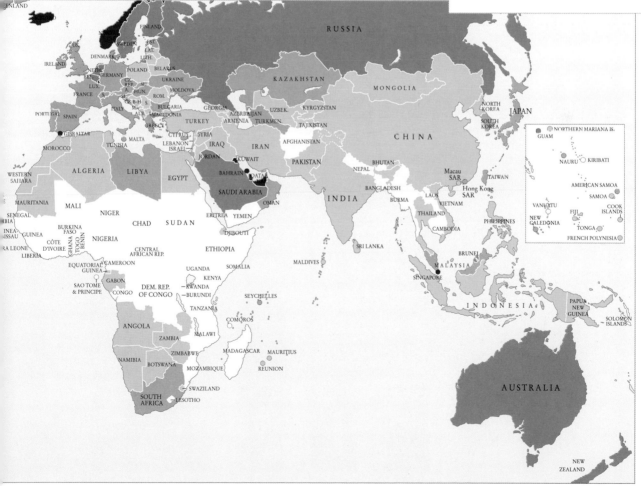

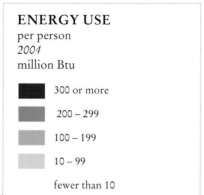

ENERGY POLICY

Despite its self-sufficiency in some fuels, America's dependence on oil means that a significant proportion of its energy supply will continue to come from overseas.

The principal criticism of National Energy Policy under President George W. Bush is that it is dictated by the needs of the energy-related industries, and energy producers in particular, rather than by the interests of consumers, or even of the planet.

If current trends continue there will a shortfall of over 40 percent in the USA's energy supply by 2020, with only 30 percent of oil needs being met by domestic supply. The policy options following on from this are the subject of heated debate. The Bush administration's main concern is to protect economic growth, whereas its critics emphasize the need to reduce the demand for energy; the administration wants to promote better technology in oil, coal and nuclear, whereas its critics want to develop new renewable energy technologies; the administration insists on protecting the interests of the big energy corporations by making policies voluntary and the industry self-regulating, whereas critics demand mandatory policies.

Nearly a third of US land is federal-owned, and previously protected areas are now being considered for exploitation by energy corporations. Those who put a premium on protecting the country's wildlife argue that improving the quality of tires on US vehicles would save more energy than opening up the Arctic Refuge. The administration argues that by mobilizing market forces it can both consume more and pollute less.

The objective of keeping access to ever-more diverse sources of supply is a lynchpin of American trade and foreign policy. It also means that the USA has a vital interest in an effective and efficient global energy infrastructure, maintaining energy security not just for itself but for other countries too, because any major disruption will affect broader foreign policy objectives, regardless of its own dependency.

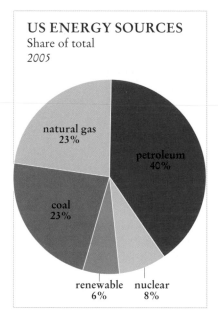

US ENERGY SOURCES
Share of total
2005

natural gas
23%

petroleum
40%

coal
23%

renewable
6%

nuclear
8%

INCREASING ENERGY USE
in the USA *1950–2005*
billion Btu

34.6 — 1950
45.0 — 1960
67.8 — 1970
78.3 — 1980
84.7 — 1990
99.9 — 2000

NUCLEAR ENERGY

The proportion of US electricity produced by nuclear power was negligible until 1970 and then grew rapidly over the next 15 years. By the 1990s it was around 20 percent. Growth was halted temporarily by widespread fears among the public after the meltdown at Three Mile Island, Pennsylvania in 1979. And it has hardly grown as a proportion of total energy use since the deadly explosion at the Chernobyl nuclear plant in the Ukraine (then part of the USSR) in 1986.

Even though nuclear power provides only one fifth of US energy needs, the USA is by far the world's largest supplier and consumer, using almost twice as much commercial nuclear power as the next country, France.

A nuclear future
In 2005 there were 103 commercial nuclear generating units in the USA, but none has been commissioned since 1978. This may be about to change. The increasing price of alternative sources of energy, notably oil, is driving a revival of the nuclear industry. Equally important is the contribution nuclear energy can make to reducing the carbon dioxide emissions from fossil fuels – the primary cause of global warming.

Objections to nuclear power remain strong: the problems of cost, waste disposal, safety, vulnerability to terrorism, and the link to nuclear weapons. None of these has an easy solution, but fossil fuels are increasingly costly, more and more difficult to access, finite in supply, environmentally damaging, and less than fully secure or safe.

On balance, it is likely that nuclear power will play an increasing role in resolving problems of energy supply, irrespective of whether the USA is able to reduce its massive demand for energy. If this makes the USA more self-sufficient, relieving the pressure for it to secure overseas oil supplies, it may have a significant impact on US foreign policy. If, on the other hand, the growth of nuclear power accelerates the proliferation of nuclear weapons, or results in a catastrophic accident or terrorist attack, it could lead US foreign policy into uncharted waters.

NUCLEAR ENERGY WORLDWIDE
Countries' share of total nuclear power consumption
2004

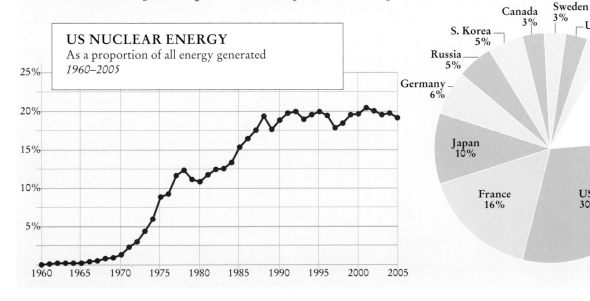

US NUCLEAR ENERGY
As a proportion of all energy generated
1960–2005

CLIMATE CHANGE

As the country emitting most carbon dioxide, the USA has been, and looks set to remain, the largest contributor to global warming.

The Kyoto Protocol to the UN Framework Convention on Climate Change requires participating countries collectively to reduce CO_2 emissions by 5.2 percent by 2012. The 1997 agreement was signed by President Clinton but never ratified by the US Senate.

The administration of George W. Bush supports the aims and principles of the Kyoto Protocol, but objects to the exemptions given to such major carbon emitters as China and India. It argues that the targets are precipitous and, in practice, would require a 30 percent reduction in US emissions and cause a cut of up to 4 percent in US GDP. It is unwilling to support any policy that puts Americans out of work.

Although there is a certain amount of support for Kyoto within the USA, with several states and cities adopting their own Kyoto-style legal limits on greenhouse gas emissions, the attitude of the Bush administration has been a prime example of US unilateralism. Its policy puts the US national interest, and even the profits of particular industries, before the global interest. The decision to adopt carbon intensity, rather than total carbon emissions, as a way of measuring emissions (*see left*) is a convenient way to protect the privileged US standard of living at the expense of the planet.

Bush argues that the best way to meet the common goal of stabilizing climate change is to promote clean and affordable technologies. The US federal budget devoted $6.5 billion in 2006 to developing technologies for using coal, hydrogen, nuclear fusion and renewables as sources of clean energy. It also developed a range of tax incentives for companies to develop market-based solutions to curb greenhouse gas emissions. This investment in new technologies, while worthy in itself, is a money-making scheme for energy corporations that does little or nothing to help poorer countries gain access to energy or lift themselves out of poverty.

The US response to Kyoto demonstrates how the USA can play by its own rules in international affairs and, in the final analysis, make the rules for others, since the rest of the world cannot act effectively without its cooperation. The US position is often justified as benign hegemony on the grounds that there has to be leader if shared problems are to be solved. Climate change is a shared problem above all others, and America's way of dealing with it to date has not been constructive.

EMISSIONS AND INTENSITY

CO_2 emissions compared with carbon intensity
2003

 CO_2 emissions in millions of metric tonnes

carbon intensity: tonnes of CO_2 emitted per $1,000 of GDP

In 2002, the USA committed to reduce its carbon intensity (the ratio of carbon emissions to GDP) by 18% by 2012 or 1.95% per year. This target has been met with a 2.3% cut in 2004 and 2.5% in 2005. However, since its GDP continues to expand this voluntary target allows America to continue to increase the absolute volume of its carbon emissions.

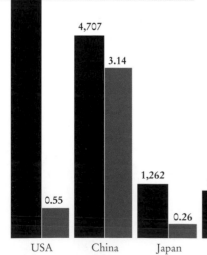

USA	5,912	0.55
China	4,707	3.14
Japan	1,262	0.26
India	1,113	1.88
UK	580	0.36
France	406	0.29
Brazil	337	0.51

66 ...ON THE ISSUE OF CLIMATE CHANGE...ECONOMIC GROWTH IS THE SOLUTION, NOT THE PROBLEM. 99

PRESIDENT GEORGE W. BUSH, FEBRUARY 2002

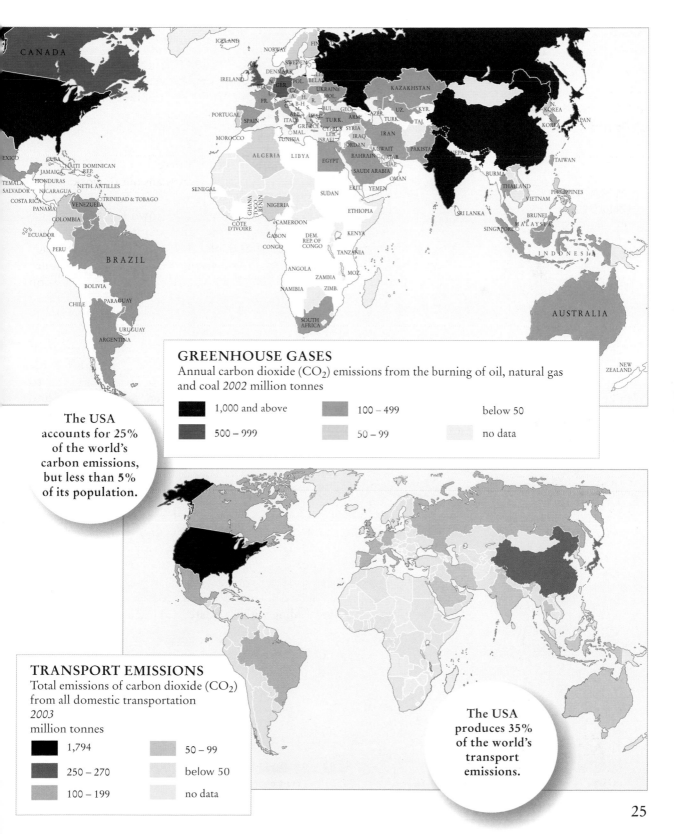

GREENHOUSE GASES

Annual carbon dioxide (CO_2) emissions from the burning of oil, natural gas and coal *2002* million tonnes

- 1,000 and above
- 500 – 999
- 100 – 499
- 50 – 99
- below 50
- no data

The USA accounts for 25% of the world's carbon emissions, but less than 5% of its population.

TRANSPORT EMISSIONS

Total emissions of carbon dioxide (CO_2) from all domestic transportation *2003* million tonnes

- 1,794
- 250 – 270
- 100 – 199
- 50 – 99
- below 50
- no data

The USA produces 35% of the world's transport emissions.

25

ENERGY SECURITY

America imports 60% of its oil, amounting to over
13 million barrels a day. By 2030 this dependency is
projected to rise to 75%, so the need to secure supplies
in a potentially hostile world will continue to drive
US foreign policy.

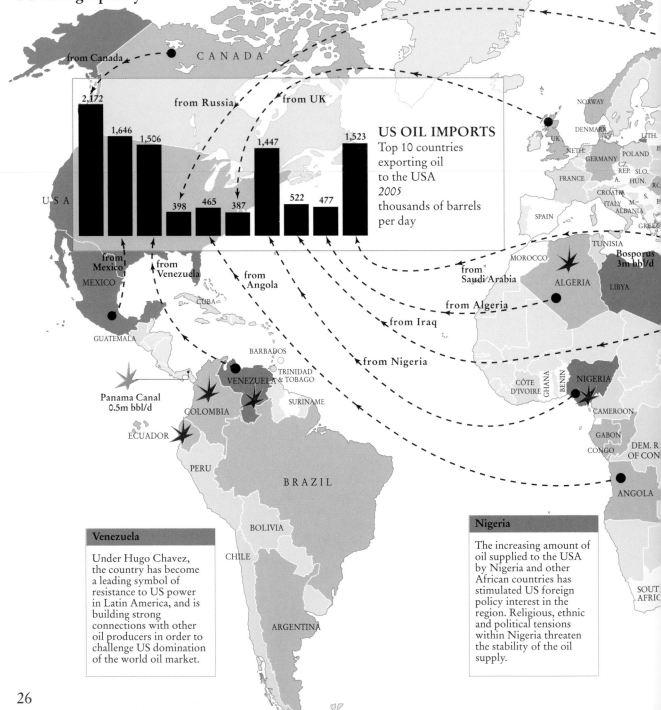

US OIL IMPORTS
Top 10 countries
exporting oil
to the USA
2005
thousands of barrels
per day

2,172

1,646

1,506

398

465

387

1,447

522

477

1,523

from Canada

from Russia

from UK

from Mexico

from Venezuela

from Angola

from Saudi Arabia

from Algeria

from Iraq

from Nigeria

Panama Canal
0.5m bbl/d

Bosporus
3m bbl/d

Venezuela

Under Hugo Chavez,
the country has become
a leading symbol of
resistance to US power
in Latin America, and is
building strong
connections with other
oil producers in order to
challenge US domination
of the world oil market.

Nigeria

The increasing amount of
oil supplied to the USA
by Nigeria and other
African countries has
stimulated US foreign
policy interest in the
region. Religious, ethnic
and political tensions
within Nigeria threaten
the stability of the oil
supply.

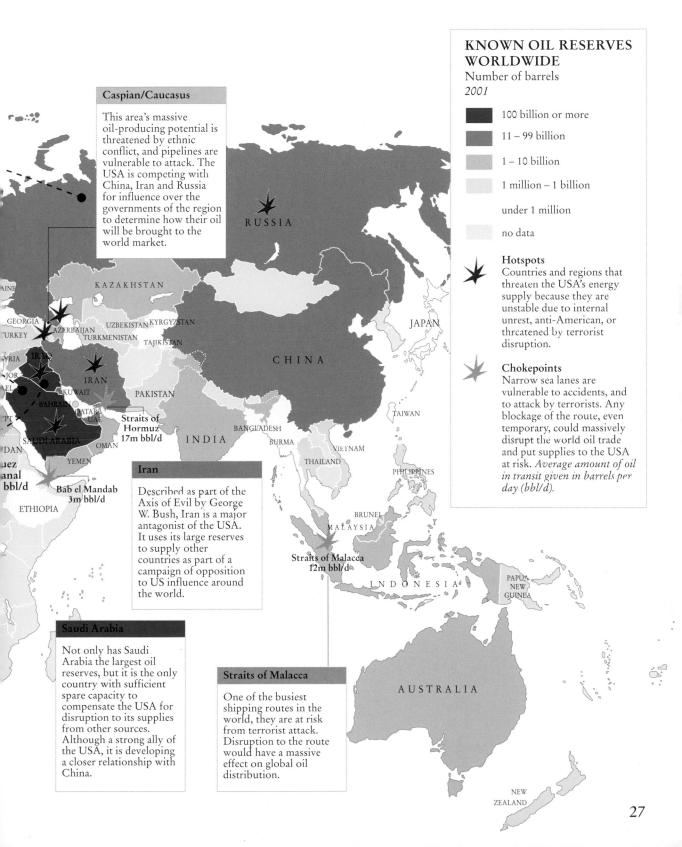

KNOWN OIL RESERVES WORLDWIDE
Number of barrels
2001

- 100 billion or more
- 11 – 99 billion
- 1 – 10 billion
- 1 million – 1 billion
- under 1 million
- no data

Hotspots
Countries and regions that threaten the USA's energy supply because they are unstable due to internal unrest, anti-American, or threatened by terrorist disruption.

Chokepoints
Narrow sea lanes are vulnerable to accidents, and to attack by terrorists. Any blockage of the route, even temporary, could massively disrupt the world oil trade and put supplies to the USA at risk. *Average amount of oil in transit given in barrels per day (bbl/d).*

Caspian/Caucasus

This area's massive oil-producing potential is threatened by ethnic conflict, and pipelines are vulnerable to attack. The USA is competing with China, Iran and Russia for influence over the governments of the region to determine how their oil will be brought to the world market.

Iran

Described as part of the Axis of Evil by George W. Bush, Iran is a major antagonist of the USA. It uses its large reserves to supply other countries as part of a campaign of opposition to US influence around the world.

Saudi Arabia

Not only has Saudi Arabia the largest oil reserves, but it is the only country with sufficient spare capacity to compensate the USA for disruption to its supplies from other sources. Although a strong ally of the USA, it is developing a closer relationship with China.

Straits of Malacca

One of the busiest shipping routes in the world, they are at risk from terrorist attack. Disruption to the route would have a massive effect on global oil distribution.

RUSSIA

KAZAKHSTAN

GEORGIA
AZERBAIJAN
TURKEY
UZBEKISTAN
KYRGYZSTAN
TURKMENISTAN
TAJIKISTAN

SYRIA
IRAQ
IRAN
PAKISTAN
CHINA

JAPAN

JORDAN
KUWAIT
BAHRAIN
QATAR
UAE

Straits of Hormuz
17m bbl/d

SAUDI ARABIA
OMAN
YEMEN

INDIA

BANGLADESH
BURMA

TAIWAN

VIETNAM
THAILAND
PHILIPPINES

Suez Canal
bbl/d

Bab el Mandab
3m bbl/d

ETHIOPIA

BRUNEI
MALAYSIA

Straits of Malacca
12m bbl/d

INDONESIA

PAPUA NEW GUINEA

AUSTRALIA

NEW ZEALAND

OIL: CONSUMPTION AND DEPENDENCY

The USA is the world's biggest oil consumer and importer.

US OIL IMPORTS
Share of US oil imports
by country
2005
Total: 13.5 million barrels per day

Mexico 12%
Saudi Arabia 11%
Canada 16%
Venezuela 11%
other 14%
Nigeria 10%
UK 3%
Russia 3%
Algeria 3%
Iraq 4%
Angola 3%

The dependence of the American way of life on oil is evident not only from the sheer volume it consumes – the highest in the world – but also from its consumption per person, which outstrips that of any other comparable country and is double that of northern Europeans.

This would not have a bearing on world affairs if the USA were self-sufficient in oil. It has plentiful supplies of coal, enough to last 250 years; it is also the biggest producer of electricity from nuclear power, and consumption from this source is likely to increase. But such is its voracious appetite that nearly 60 percent of its oil, and 96 percent of the oil Americans use for transport, has to be imported. There is no prospect of the need for imported oil declining in the foreseeable future; indeed, all projections forecast an increase.

America has not been self-sufficient in oil since the 1950s. When the USA's domestic production of petroleum peaked at over 11 million barrels a day in 1970, net imports stood at just over 3 million. As domestic supply declined, consumption grew, and in 1996 net imports surpassed domestic supply for the first time. By 2005, imports had far outstripped domestic production.

The USA continues to be the world's biggest importer of oil, accounting for around one quarter of total world imports. While the USA, like most other oil-importing countries, is reliant on supplies from the Middle East, which holds the majority of the world's oil reserves, the political instability of the Middle East, and the threat this carries to supply, has led US policy-makers to look closer to home. In

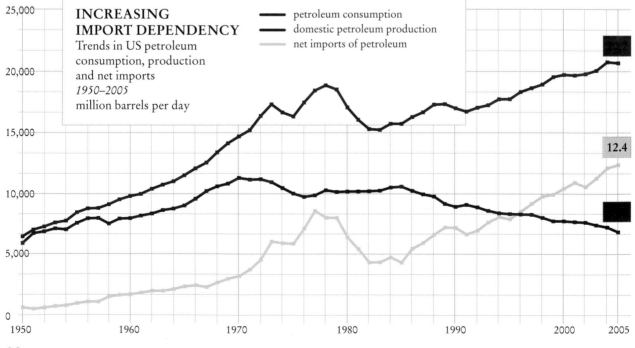

INCREASING IMPORT DEPENDENCY
Trends in US petroleum consumption, production and net imports
1950–2005
million barrels per day

— petroleum consumption
— domestic petroleum production
— net imports of petroleum

12.4

this respect the USA is in a more favorable position than many other countries. Japan and China, for example, rely on the Middle East for most of their imports.

The USA is heavily reliant on the Western Hemisphere, from which its two main suppliers are Mexico and Venezuela. Whereas Mexico sends 80 percent of its oil output to the USA, and maintains close political and economical ties, Venezuela exports approximately half its production to the USA, and is actively seeking alternative markets in Asia because of its ideological differences with the Bush administration.

Even Saudi Arabia, whose national security concerns make it willing to maintain a very high profile as a supplier to the US market, has diversified its exports in order to feed the rapid growth of demand from Asia.

Although US dependence on the Middle East has declined, this has not made the USA less vulnerable to rising costs. Since oil is a single, global market, prices are determined by the world balance between supply and demand. Demand is growing rapidly, especially from Asia, and so prices are rising for everyone.

To obtain the best price and to protect itself from becoming too dependent on a single country, the USA attempts to diversify its sources of oil. From a US perspective, supplies are always subject to uncertainty. Not only are they limited by the quantity and quality of reserves, they are also subject to the vagaries of the political process in each country. Because oil is a global product, the USA's high consumption and dependency means it must act globally to secure supplies. Its interest in guaranteeing plentiful supplies of oil translates into the need to secure access to virtually every region in the world, and this explains why oil has such a widespread effect on America's global political strategy.

> " FOR TOO LONG OUR NATION HAS BEEN DEPENDENT ON FOREIGN OIL. AND THIS DEPENDENCE LEAVES US MORE VULNERABLE TO HOSTILE REGIMES, AND TO TERRORISTS. "
>
> PRESIDENT GEORGE W. BUSH
> STATE OF THE UNION
> JANUARY 23, 2007

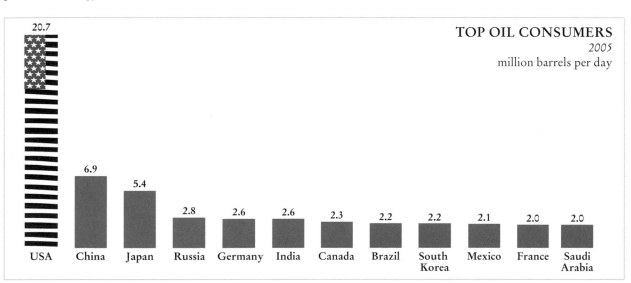

TOP OIL CONSUMERS
2005
million barrels per day

USA	China	Japan	Russia	Germany	India	Canada	Brazil	South Korea	Mexico	France	Saudi Arabia
20.7	6.9	5.4	2.8	2.6	2.6	2.3	2.2	2.2	2.1	2.0	2.0

OIL POLICY

No single oil-rich country is indispensable to the USA.

HALLIBURTON

1989 President George Bush inaugurated. Dick Cheney is Defense Secretary and Halliburton, one of the biggest oil-services companies in the world, wins a five-year contract to provide logistics for the US Army.

1993 President Bill Clinton inaugurated. Cheney leaves office to become CEO of Halliburton.

1996–98 With Cheney as CEO, Halliburton jumps from 73rd to 18th on the Pentagon's list of top contractors, receiving contracts worth at least $3.8 billion.

1997–2000 Halliburton has stakes in two firms contracted to sell over $73 million in oil-production equipment to Iraq and contravenes US ban to deal with Libya and Iran.

2000 Cheney resigns from Halliburton but continues to receive up to $1 million per annum.

2001 President George W. Bush inaugurated. Dick Cheney becomes Vice-President, and after 9/11, Halliburton wins defense contracts worth over $2.2 billion.

2002 Halliburton consulted about post-war oil production in Iraq.

2003 Halliburton subsidiary, Kellogg Brown and Root (KBR) contracted to extinguish oil well fires in Iraq, and supports operations in Afghanistan, Djibouti, Georgia, Jordan, and Uzbekistan. Halliburton wins billion-dollar contract to work alongside US troops in Kuwait and Turkey.

2004 Halliburton awarded contracts worth $18 billion to rebuild Iraq; KBR receives at least $3.9 billion to rebuild in Iraq and Afghanistan.

The interests of domestic oil producers have always influenced US foreign policy. Rarely, however, has the oil industry and its political lobby enjoyed as much influence as during the administration of George W. Bush, as is shown by the case of the Halliburton Company, formerly led by Vice-President Cheney.

The key to US overseas oil policy is to improve the security of supply by diversifying the sources from which it gets its oil. Saudi Arabia has the largest proven reserves *(see pages 26–27)*, so it is not surprising that the USA maintains close ties with the Saudi regime.

Along with the United Arab Emirates, the next largest reserves are in Iraq, and a continued US presence there would make those supplies as secure as any in the world. Although not necessarily the main motivation for US intervention in the country, it is hard to believe that it was not a factor in the Bush administrations' calculations.

Although the USA has longer-term plans to create a more stable Middle East through extending democratic government, its own military presence and its support for Israel, together with the internal strains in the Middle East, make the region unstable, and jeopardize the long-term availability of oil from this source.

Russia has the next largest reserves and is dependent on selling oil and gas to finance its economic resurgence. Russia's main market is not the USA, but Europe. However, since the USA and Europe have similar interests, closer ties between Russia and Europe are part of a common enterprise of diversifying supply, rather than a source of contention between the USA and Europe.

In Russia's backyard, but tantalizingly out of its control, lie the large oil reserves of the Caspian Sea. US influence, evident in the growth of US military intervention and bases across the region, is not welcomed by Russia, and the Caspian has the potential to become a flashpoint as the world superpower and its former great rival battle for influence.

Oil from Latin America is becoming increasingly important. Despite its domination of its own hemisphere, the USA has not succeeded in overthrowing the left-wing regime in Venezuela, a sign of the limits of its power. When the USA is rebuffed in one region, however, true to the nature of its global reach, it seeks control in other areas. Since the Cold War, increased pressures on the world's supplies of oil have led to a greater US interest in countries such as Angola and Nigeria. This interest has been manifested in aid, either sent direct or via agencies such as the World Bank, with loans linked to the capacity to extract natural resources.

As long as the world oil market remains diverse and global in character no single oil-rich region or country is indispensable to the USA. Consequently, and to this end, it retains a great deal of flexibility in wider foreign policy objectives. Should the geopolitics of the oil market change, however, then the USA may face more acute policy dilemmas.

THE GEOPOLITICS OF OIL

As America's oil dependency increases, it creates pressures that run counter to the main thrust of its foreign policy and wider imperial standing. To ensure supplies, the USA has to import its oil either from autocratic states, like Saudi Arabia; anti-American countries such as Venezuela; places beyond its control like Russia; or from somewhere embodying all of these, like Iran.

The countries with the largest oil reserves are Saudi Arabia (259 billion barrels) and Iraq (112 billion barrels)

America's dependence makes it vulnerable to a possible alliance between these countries denying it access to world oil markets. The real threat arises when oil-rich countries collaborate with fast-growing consumers, such as China and India. World oil flows are changing to reflect this new network of energy suppliers and consumers, and together they have the potential to strangle America's access to oil.

China is at the heart of this threat. Well-placed and widely predicted to develop into a superpower, it has the potential to lead a network of alliances that will challenge US hegemony. China's oil imports are expected to grow fourfold by 2030 and, in order to secure its supplies, it is developing closer relations with anti-American regimes, such as Venezuela and Iran. Moreover, China's status as a permanent member of the UN Security Council gives it the power to protect its friends by vetoing US policies – on, for example, nuclear proliferation and human rights – and restraining US foreign policy well beyond the realm of oil.

The USA faces two choices. It can act, with force if necessary, to create more amenable regimes; Iraq is the prime example of this, with Venezuela and Iran ripe for consideration. This a dramatic and dangerous policy but fostering regime change is not new to the USA, albeit dressed up as part of the struggle against the axis of evil, in which increased access to oil is a happy consequence of taking the moral high ground. The alternative is to secure supplies by supporting authoritarian regimes. The USA has a history of supping with the devil: in the Cold War the struggle against communism was used to justify alliances with all manner of barbaric regimes, and oil is no less vital a driver of American foreign policy.

In practice, US policy will be a combination of both options, but the recipe for conflict is potent because of deep-rooted resistance to US power by the new oil-rich producers and new oil-hungry consumers. These countries are motivated not only by a desire to further their own national interests, but also to challenge the massively unequal global distribution of wealth that has the USA at its peak.

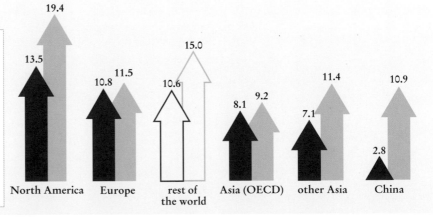

FUTURE US OIL IMPORTS
by region
2030 compared with 2003
million barrels per day
2003

2003

2030

19.4
13.5
North America

10.8 11.5
Europe

15.0
10.6
rest of the world

8.1 9.2
Asia (OECD)

7.1 11.4
other Asia

2.8 10.9
China

Chapter Two
TRADE

After World War II, the USA became the major architect and driving force of a global free-trade regime. Its foreign policy was initially directed towards building a bulwark against communist expansion through a system of free trade between capitalist states. During the Cold War and the subsequent post-communist age of globalization, the USA has remained committed to the notion that free trade is not only the key to prosperity but also to democracy and peace, dependent as this is on an orderly exchange of goods and services. The principles that have guided the US policy of liberalization have been those of equal treatment for all countries in respect of tariffs, the so-called "most favored nation" principle, and transparency in the rules governing the conduct of trade without regulation or subsidy. Its free-trade approach has helped to create prosperity among the more developed economies, although the gap between rich and poor countries has widened.

Free trade has not received universal support in the USA. Even if it produces more efficiency overall, some groups are bound to suffer as the international division of labor changes, and those who feel most threatened will want state protection from against overseas competition. Many sectors of the American economy, especially manufacturing, have already felt the effect of less-developed economies overseas becoming more efficient. Workers have seen their jobs outsourced or eliminated by cheap imports, and their political representatives have led the fight against free trade. Despite these protectionist pressures, so far the liberalizing tendency has predominated.

As American foreign policy has become more aggressive and controlling under George W. Bush, the USA has curbed its commitment to free trade in order to further its wider goals; it has used the stick of trade sanctions and the carrot of trade agreements to project its values across the world and bend other countries to its will.

> "WE'RE MAKING SURE AMERICA HAS A CHANCE TO COMPETE ON THE SAME TERMS AS PEOPLE WHO SELL INTO OUR MARKET. AND WE'LL USE THE TOOLS NECESSARY TO MAKE SURE THE PLAYING FIELD IS LEVEL."
>
> PRESIDENT GEORGE W. BUSH
> 2004

IMBALANCE OF TRADE

The USA was once self-sufficient, but since the 1970s it has run a trade deficit.

Since the 1970s, as the USA has become more integrated into the world economy, it has run a trade deficit, importing more goods than it has exported. This seems unusual for an imperial power, but US trade policy is not altruistic: trade deficits support the US standard of living by providing cheap goods. Free trade also gives America access to export markets, helps keep inflation low, and has led to a high rate of economic growth since the 1990s.

Imbalances in trade are also used to achieve wider foreign policy goals. China is developing very fast and its potential is obvious. Successive US administrations have dealt with this emerging rival by attempting to make China's prosperity dependent on a constructive relationship with the world economy. By supporting China's admission to the World Trade Organization, the USA ensured that it accept the rules of international trade.

In the same way as it dealt with Japan after the war, the USA has run a massive trade deficit with China. It is a relationship of mutual

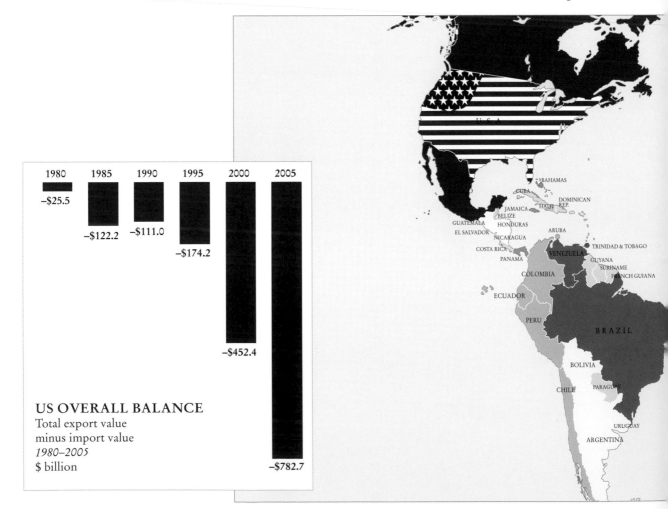

1980	1985	1990	1995	2000	2005
−$25.5	−$122.2	−$111.0	−$174.2	−$452.4	−$782.7

US OVERALL BALANCE
Total export value
minus import value
1980–2005
$ billion

advantage: the deficit increases the supply of goods for US consumers at a price that curbs inflation, and it makes China dependent on the US market. However, the economic interests of the USA and China do not converge completely. China is making alliances with other countries in the Middle East, Latin America and Africa to secure supplies of raw materials, bringing it into direct competition with the USA.

The trade deficit also allows China to build massive dollar reserves, now exceeding $600 billion. Much of this is invested in US Treasury bonds. This helps strengthen mutual dependence, but increasingly China is using its reserves to buy US companies. When Japan did something similar in the 1980s the American reaction was strong and openly racist. China is a bigger potential threat, and if it continues on this path, the economic ties cultivated by the USA may not be sufficient to prevent open conflict.

US BALANCE OF TRADE
2005
US$ millions

US trade deficit

- $50,000 and above
- $5,000 – $30,000
- $1,000 – $4,999
- below $1,000

US trade surplus

- below $1,000
- $1,000 and above
- no data

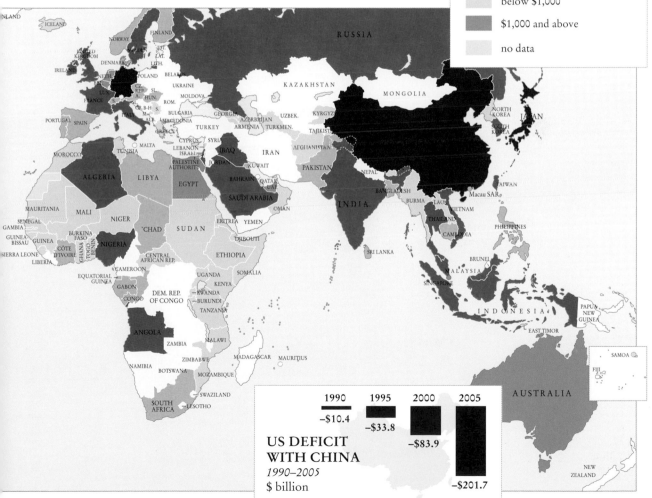

	1990	1995	2000	2005
	−$10.4	−$33.8	−$83.9	−$201.7

US DEFICIT WITH CHINA
1990–2005
$ billion

TRADING PARTNERS

The USA uses its power to extend its markets by ensuring preferential trading relationships with other countries.

The USA is dependent on the world economy for its prosperity, and an unregulated world market poses as serious a threat to America's national security as armed aggression. To secure its position, the USA has used its political influence to extract preferential trading relations with other countries.

The USA's membership of regional economic associations demonstrates its unique position as a power involved in every major region, and ensures that it is not left exposed in the event of a collapse in the global economy. The North American Free Trade Agreement (NAFTA) gives American-based capital access to cheaper labor, and has integrated Mexico into the world economy on US terms. In 1994, the USA proposed a Free Trade Area of the Americas (FTAA), but this has still not been negotiated because of resistance from Latin American countries, and from within the USA.

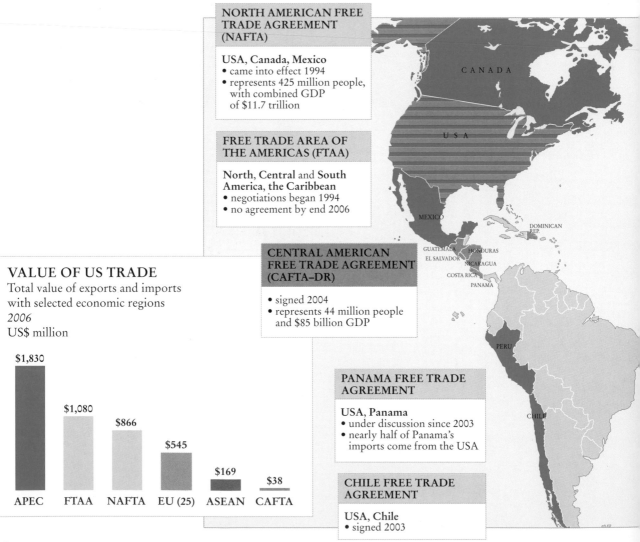

NORTH AMERICAN FREE TRADE AGREEMENT (NAFTA)

USA, Canada, Mexico
• came into effect 1994
• represents 425 million people, with combined GDP of $11.7 trillion

FREE TRADE AREA OF THE AMERICAS (FTAA)

North, Central and South America, the Caribbean
• negotiations began 1994
• no agreement by end 2006

CENTRAL AMERICAN FREE TRADE AGREEMENT (CAFTA–DR)

• signed 2004
• represents 44 million people and $85 billion GDP

PANAMA FREE TRADE AGREEMENT

USA, Panama
• under discussion since 2003
• nearly half of Panama's imports come from the USA

CHILE FREE TRADE AGREEMENT

USA, Chile
• signed 2003

VALUE OF US TRADE
Total value of exports and imports with selected economic regions
2006
US$ million

APEC	$1,830
FTAA	$1,080
NAFTA	$866
EU (25)	$545
ASEAN	$169
CAFTA	$38

The countries of Asia are a source of cheap manufactured products and a potential consumer market that dwarfs all others. APEC may become the most significant of all regional associations because of the size and dynamism of this area – its members account for half of world trade – but the USA is having difficulty retaining leadership as Asian countries, led by China, are increasingly acting alone.

The USA's strongest economic relationship is with Europe. But the dividing line between partnership and rivalry is murky, and there have been disputes over trade issues. A transatlantic free-trade area (TAFTA) has been proposed to prevent economic rivalry getting out of hand, but there are concerns that it could appear as an exclusive club for rich countries, and it has failed to get beyond the planning stage. Transatlantic tariffs averaging 3.5 percent are, in any case, so low as to make an agreement superfluous.

US TRADE AGREEMENTS
2006

Members of:

- Asia–Pacific Economic Cooperation (APEC)
- Association of South-East Asian Nations (ASEAN)
- Central American Free Trade Agreement (CAFTA)
- Middle East Free Trade Area (MEFTA)
- other countries

APEC
- established 1989
- 21 economies representing over 2.6 billion people and 47% of world trade

SOUTH KOREA FREE TRADE AGREEMENT

USA, South Korea
- negotiated 2007 with USA's seventh largest partner
- comprehensive agreement covering agriculture and services as well as nearly all manufactured trade
- protects US investors in South Korea

MOROCCO FREE TRADE AGREEMENT

USA, Morocco
- signed 2004
- an attempt to build a closer relationship with a force for moderation in the Islamic world

ISRAEL FREE TRADE AGREEMENT

USA, Israel
- signed 1985
- oldest bilateral agreement, with America's staunchest ally

MIDDLE EAST FREE TRADE AREA (MEFTA)
- proposed by the Bush Administration in 2003
- aim to establish by 2013
- billed as part of a plan to fight terrorism by supporting the growth of democracy through trade

ASEAN
- USA's fifth largest trading partner
- represents 537 million people with a GDP of $679 billion

OMAN FREE TRADE AGREEMENT
- signed 2006
- secures a $1 billion two-way trade relationship

BAHRAIN FREE TRADE AGREEMENT

USA, Bahrain
- signed 2004

SINGAPORE FREE TRADE AGREEMENT

USA, Singapore
- signed 2003
- will serve as the foundation for other FTAs in South-East Asia under ASEAN

JORDAN FREE TRADE AGREEMENT

USA, Jordan
- signed 2000
- USA's first trade agreement with an Arab state

AUSTRALIAN FREE TRADE AGREEMENT (AUSFTA)

USA, Australia
- signed 2004

GLOBAL TRADE

The USA helped set up the World Trade Organization, and uses its mechanisms to maintain a strong hold on world trade.

Since World War II, the value of international trade has increased by a factor of 20. The driving force behind such a heady expansion was, in the first instance, the General Agreement on Tariffs and Trade (GATT). In 1995, GATT's role was taken over by the World Trade Organization (WTO), now the only international organization overseeing rules of trade between nations. Its main function is to ensure that trade flows as smoothly, predictably and freely as possible.

The USA played a major role in drawing up the rules that guide the WTO. This helps explain why, despite its usual reluctance to recognize the authority of international bodies, it has been willing to abide by WTO rulings. In fact, the USA has used the WTO dispute mechanism more than any other country in the world.

The WTO has been heavily criticized for favoring multinational corporations that sacrifice environmental and labor considerations to the pursuit of profit, leading to even greater global inequality. Its creation has crystallized opposition to globalization, vividly realized at the December 1999 meeting of the WTO in Seattle, when a coalition of demonstrators matched the number of official delegates.

Although the architecture and rules of the WTO tend to favor developed economies, its rulings do not always favor the USA. The risk is that if the USA finds the WTO turning against its interests, it may withdraw co-operation and rely instead on its bilateral and regional network – a course that would put the global free-trade infrastructure in jeopardy.

WORLD TRADE ORGANIZATION
1996–2006

- member of the WTO
- other countries

Number of WTO disputes in which country has been complainant
1996 – 2006

- 70 or more
- 10 – 30

THE BANANA DISPUTE

The trade dispute between the EU and the USA over bananas reveals how wealthy corporations can hijack US foreign policy. Bananas would barely rate on the broader canvass of US foreign affairs, but a number of US corporations, most notably Chiquita, dominate the international banana market, and therefore care a great deal about the issue. Their lobbying of US politicians, and their large contributions to political funds, resulted in the USA becoming embroiled in a long-running WTO dispute to protect their commercial interests.

The dispute

The industrial-scale production methods of the multinationals enable them to produce some of the cheapest bananas on the world market, and they dominate the world banana trade. In 1993, the European Union sought to protect small-scale banana producers in its former colonies in Africa and the Caribbean (the ACP countries) by imposing tariffs and quotas on bananas imported from other countries.

The USA, persuaded of the need to protect its commercial interests in Central and Latin America, complained to the WTO in 1995, in conjunction with other countries affected by the tariffs. A dispute procedure was put in place that stretched over six years. During that time the USA was granted leave to impose import duties totaling $191 million on goods from EU countries, damaging many European small businesses.

The ruling

In 2001, the WTO brokered an uneasy settlement. Following a transition period, which ended in 2005, the EU is allowed to import a duty-free quota of 775,000 tonnes of bananas from ACP suppliers, with all other banana imports attracting a tariff. In 2006, the EU set the tariff at €176 per tonne, but this is considered by some countries to be too high, and further complaints to the WTO are likely.

Fair Trade *vs* Free Trade

The banana dispute demonstrates how the WTO mechanism is used by those involved in the broader geopolitical power struggle, but provides no protection for the interests and livelihoods of small-scale farmers. The bulk of the profit in the banana trade goes to the multinationals and the supermarkets. For independent growers it is fair trade that matters, not free trade.

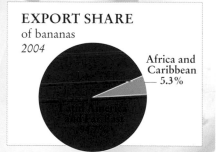

EXPORT SHARE
of bananas
2004

Africa and Caribbean — 5.3%

Latin America and Far East 94.7%

USA

JAMAICA
BELIZE
GUATEMALA
HONDURAS
NICARAGUA
COSTA RICA
PANAMA
DOMINICAN REP
ST VINCENT & GRENAD
ST LUCIA
DOMINICA
GRENADA
SURINAME
ECUADOR

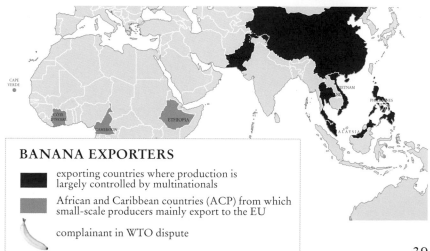

CAPE VERDE
CÔTE D'IVOIRE
CAMEROON
ETHIOPIA
VIETNAM
PHILIPPINES
MALAYSIA

BANANA EXPORTERS

- ▇ exporting countries where production is largely controlled by multinationals
- ▇ African and Caribbean countries (ACP) from which small-scale producers mainly export to the EU
- 🍌 complainant in WTO dispute

TRADE AND FOREIGN POLICY

Trade policy is an essential element of US foreign policy because economic security is vital to national security.

Since the end of the Cold War, the USA has used trade policy as a vehicle for asserting its power. While claiming to establish an international economic system that would ensure stability and prosperity for all, it has also ensured continued US domination. By conceiving a strategy that merged these two goals, the USA demonstrated that it plays by different rules from those of the rest of the world.

As part of this strategy the USA has constructed a new global division of labor. It has farmed out less-advanced activities, such as mass production of artefacts and lower-level services, to other countries, while itself embracing rapid technological development that underpins its economic dynamism and keeps it ahead of the rest of the world. However, even though it now sits at the apex of the world economy, this division of labor makes it vulnerable. During the Cold War, the USA was connected to the rest of the world primarily for strategic reasons, and its economy was relatively self-sufficient, but in the era of globalization the ties have been inverted, and the standard of living of average Americans now depends on the relationship between the USA and the world economy.

The task facing America's political leaders has therefore been reconfigured. In the Cold War their role was to manage the domestic inequality produced by industrial capitalism alongside international strategic relationships resulting from the conflict with communism. Today, the strategic dimension has been downgraded, and the main task is to manage both the domestic and international economies; these tasks have merged into one, as protecting and promoting the interests of powerful domestic industries, such as agriculture, can only be achieved by an effective foreign trade policy.

IMPORTANCE OF TRADE
Value of trade as
percentage of GDP
1976–2004

SUBSIDIES: THE EXAMPLE OF COTTON

The USA accounts for nearly half of all cotton exports, and sells its cotton for around half what it costs to produce it, thanks to enormous US government subsidies. This trade practice – known as "dumping" – is a reflection of the formidable power wielded by the National Cotton Council in protecting the interests of large US farmers. Their lobbying obtained beneficial treatment for cotton in successive US farm bills, culminating in the 2002 bill, which clearly favored the Texas cotton barons.

Industrial-sized farms have typically collected annual payments in excess of $1 million, although smaller farmers in the USA, in common with those elsewhere in the world, are being driven out of business by the low prices. In Africa, more than 10 million people directly depend on cotton exports for their livelihood. In Mali and Benin, the loss endured by the import of subsidized US cotton is estimated to exceed US aid to these countries. The recent decline in world cotton prices is responsible for a 4 percent increase in national poverty in these countries.

WTO judgement

In September 2004, a WTO dispute panel, in a case brought by Brazil, supported by Argentina, Australia, Benin, Chad, China, the European Union and several other countries, found that $3.2 billion in annual cotton subsidies, and $1.6 billion in export credits paid by the USA, were illegal under WTO rules. The US appeal against the ruling was rejected, and the USA is supposed to be complying with the ruling.

Poor countries are continually told that their salvation lies in trade not aid. The realities of the world cotton market demonstrate how the USA preaches the merits of open trade but destroys trade opportunities for poor countries and reinforces unequal patterns of globalization. The WTO case is a test, the outcome of which may encourage poorer countries to use the WTO to create fairer trade by attacking the subsidies rich countries give to their agriculture. Unless the USA and other rich countries respond in a positive way, the prospects for the reform of world agriculture are poor.

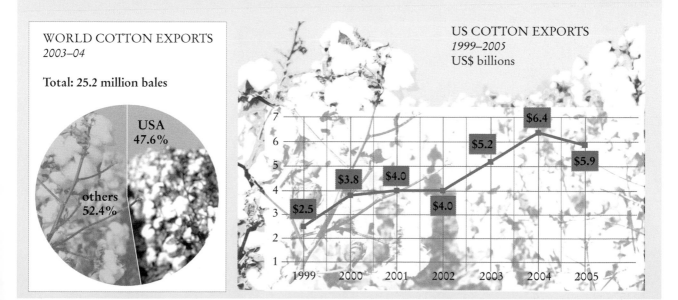

WORLD COTTON EXPORTS
2003–04

Total: 25.2 million bales

USA
47.6%

others
52.4%

US COTTON EXPORTS
1999–2005
US$ billions

$2.5 — $3.8 — $4.0 — $4.0 — $5.2 — $6.4 — $5.9

1999 2000 2001 2002 2003 2004 2005

Chapter Three

CAPITAL

The movement of capital complements the trading of goods and services in international economic relations. Capital can be moved in two ways: by companies owning shares in companies in other countries (equity capital), or by corporations owning or controlling the management of business enterprises in other countries (direct investment).

The use of US capital to finance commercial concerns in other countries may be of even greater importance than the management of the world trade system by the USA. Financial investment not only has a direct effect on economic growth in the receiving countries, but is cumulative. Over the years the USA has built up a significant stock of capital abroad, which gives it control over the shape of other countries' economic development.

Capital flows both ways, and the inward flow to the USA is at least as important as that from the USA overseas. Trade and capital movements are closely tied as parts of a single system; the massive US trade deficit is only sustainable because other countries purchase US Treasury securities, corporate bonds and shares in US companies, or set up branches of their own corporations in the USA. This compensating inward flow of capital balances the US international economic accounts. US dependence on this form of investment creates a degree of economic vulnerability. At the end of 2004 the value of foreign investments in the USA exceeded the value of US investments abroad by $2,156 billion – the result of years of US trade deficits being financed by a cumulative inward flow of capital.

What does this mean for US imperialism? How is it that a world superpower should not only import more goods than it sells abroad, but also cede ownership of significant elements of its own economy in order to make its books balance? In fact, this situation results in a mutual dependency between the USA and the rest of the industrialized world which makes the maintenance of the American Empire vital to all concerned.

> " CAPITAL IS DEAD LABOUR, WHICH, VAMPIRE-LIKE, LIVES ONLY BY SUCKING LIVING LABOUR, AND LIVES THE MORE, THE MORE LABOUR IT SUCKS. "
>
> KARL MARX
> POLITICAL PHILOSOPHER
> (1818–83)

INVESTMENT

The USA is surprisingly dependent on the economic co-operation of its allies and partners.

Capital flows have become increasingly significant to the USA as it has become more integrated into the world economy. An increasing number of American jobs, and a growing proportion of profits of US corporations, depend on foreign investment. But the USA is living beyond its means, with more dollars being invested in companies and projects overseas than are being invested by overseas companies in the USA. This net outflow of investment, when added to the trade deficit, creates a level of economic vulnerability that makes the US surprisingly dependent on the goodwill and economic cooperation of its allies and partners.

USA–Asia

The sizeable inflow of investment from Asia comes mainly from Japan, as it finds a home for the dollars created by its long-standing trade surplus with the USA. The massive trade surplus that China is now developing is also creating capital, which it is beginning to invest in the USA. A large proportion is invested in US Treasury bonds, but Chinese economic enterprises are increasingly investing directly in US companies, arousing political sensitivities. In 2005 Congress stopped the Chinese state-run oil firm from buying the California-based Unocal Corporation, fearful that the purchase was part of a larger Chinese government strategy to lock-up future energy reserves.

CANADA

ASIA AND PACIFIC

$390.1

USA

$216.

$325.9

FOREIGN DIRECT INVESTMENT
by USA and in USA
2004 $ billions
by region

US FDI   Total: $2,242 billion

FDI in the USA   Total: $1,526 billion

The figures for foreign direct investment (FDI) do not give a complete picture of the control US capital exercises over other countries. They do not include capital raised locally in response to foreign investment, which has become an important source of finance for investment projects in some developing countries. In addition, FDI statistics underestimate the integration of the world economy, because they do not count cross-border flows of good and services within an international company.

Other countries are willing to help support the US economy in return for the guarantee of a secure economic and political environment within which the international capitalist system can operate. They collude with American imperialism, not necessarily because they all agree with every US policy decision, but because they see it as in their interest to maintain the USA as the provider of the stability and security essential to the free flow of capital, goods and services upon which international capitalism depends for its dynamism. The money they invest in the USA can, therefore, be seen as a form of imperial rent.

USA–Europe

Despite the rapid growth of many developing countries, and the gradual shift in US trade away from Europe, the North Atlantic relationship continues to dominate world capital flows. The special relationship between the UK and the USA flourishes. The UK receives almost 40% of US capital investment in Europe, and accounts for a third of European investment in the USA. It receives US investment equal to that for the whole of Latin America.

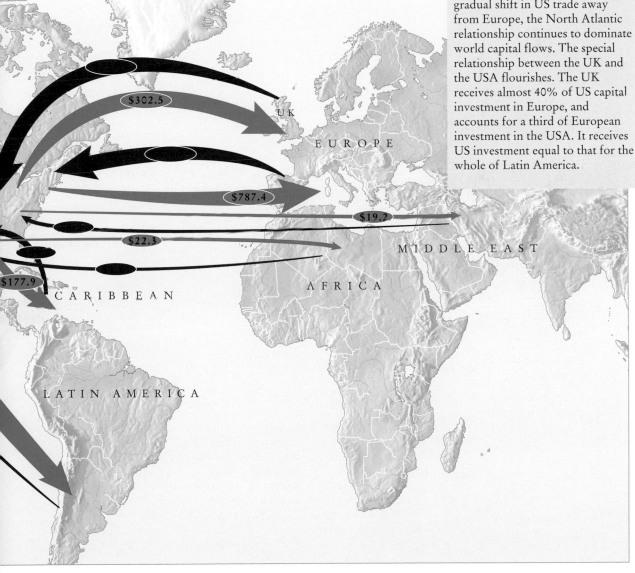

MULTINATIONALS

Over a third of the world's largest multinationals are based in the USA, and their growth is strongest in emerging markets.

Multinational corporations (MNCs) are responsible for much of the movement of capital throughout the global economy. Over a third of the 100 largest MNCs are based in the USA. Although only a quarter of the operations of these companies take place outside the USA, the proportion is rising. Overseas operations of US MNCs account for half of their profits – twice as much as would be expected from the size of their overseas production. This is largely the result of US MNCs employing an increasing number of people overseas – 8.3 million in 2004 – in countries where wage rates are much lower than in the USA. Although US consumers as a whole benefit from the reduction in the price of goods, many American workers feel threatened as they watch their jobs being exported.

Employment and investment growth is strongest in emerging markets such as China, India, Mexico, Malaysia, and Poland. Large operations can also have a critical impact even on developed economies. Over 18 percent of Ireland's economy is owned by affiliates of US MNCs. And even in countries, such as Australia, where US-owned operations generate only 5 percent of GDP, these have made way for a similar level of investment by other countries with similar interests. In the Czech Republic the situation is even more marked: only 2 percent of GDP is produced by US MNCs, but 22 percent by all MNCs.

Trade and FDI are interdependent, with US MNCs accounting for 47 percent of US exports and 37 percent of US imports. Decisions on both aspects of the economy are therefore taken by the key players in the multinational corporations.

IMPORTANCE OF MULTINATIONALS
Value added by US MNCs as percentage of GDP of host countries
2004
selected countries

- 10.0% and above
- 5.0% – 9.9%
- 1.0% – 4.9%
- below 1.0%
- no data

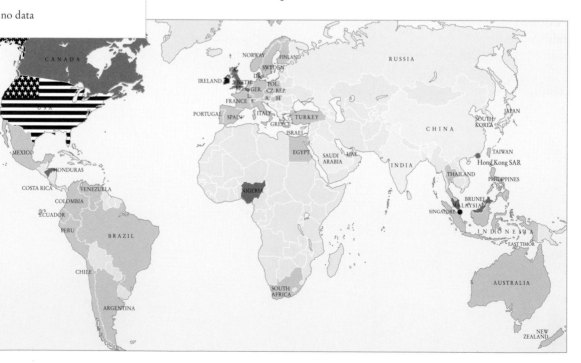

COCA-COLA

The Coca-Cola logo is one of the world's most recognized symbols, with around three-quarters of the corporation's sales being overseas. Coca-Cola has been investing heavily in emerging markets, such as China, Egypt, Pakistan and Russia. It not only establishes production facilities, but a distribution and marketing infrastructure as well. This is complemented by heavy involvement in charitable, sporting, and educational activity in local communities.

The bottling network
Coca-Cola's global impact is much greater than its relatively modest workforce suggests. Only 42 percent of the bottling plants it uses are owned by the MNC. The rest, which employ nearly 1 million people, are either independent, or minority controlled. In has thereby created a network of small business owners, who provide it with local connections, and influence with virtually every government in the world. Investment of capital is therefore the key, not just to making profit, but to insinuating Coca-Cola's, and America's, values and culture in the 200 countries in which it operates.

The bottling network also allows Coca-Cola to distance itself from ruthless labor practices. For example the company has denied any involvement in incidents in Colombia, where workers at bottling plants have been killed, tortured or kidnapped by violent paramilitaries, aided, it is alleged, by plant managements in a bid to drive down wages.

Criticism
Coca-Cola is not totally immune from criticism, however. In Poland, for example, it has been linked with increasing obesity in children, and has, as a consequence, replaced its sodas with bottled water and fruit juices in Polish elementary schools. Coca-Cola has also been the victim of its identification with American culture, and, by implication with US foreign policy. It has been the subject of an Arab boycott for many years because of its own, and America's, association with Israel.

Coca-Cola is increasingly criticized for its environmental impact. Its image in India has suffered since 2002 because of its production. Its voracious demand for water has led to water supplies drying up in several regions. The problems were compounded in Kerala: waste products from the biggest Coca-Cola plant in India that had been sold as fertilizer to local farmers were found to contain dangerous chemicals.

Total people employed: 71,000

in USA 12,200

EMPLOYEES
Number of people employed by Coca-Cola
2006

CAPITAL TRANSACTIONS

America guarantees the free flow of capital across the world's borders.

Capital flows operate through the Foreign Exchange (Forex) market, which functions "virtually", on a 24-hour basis. From 1997 to the end of 2000, daily Forex trading volume surged, from around US$5 billion to US$1.5 trillion and more, and by the end of 2005 was approaching $2.0 trillion. It thus dwarfs all other trading markets in size and volume.

The US role is not simply to export capital. Indeed, it imports more than it exports in order to finance its trade deficit. Rather, the US role is to guarantee the free flow of capital across borders to wherever it can make the greatest return.

Capital flows can only occur in a secure environment, one in which, over time, profit on investment can safely be realized and either

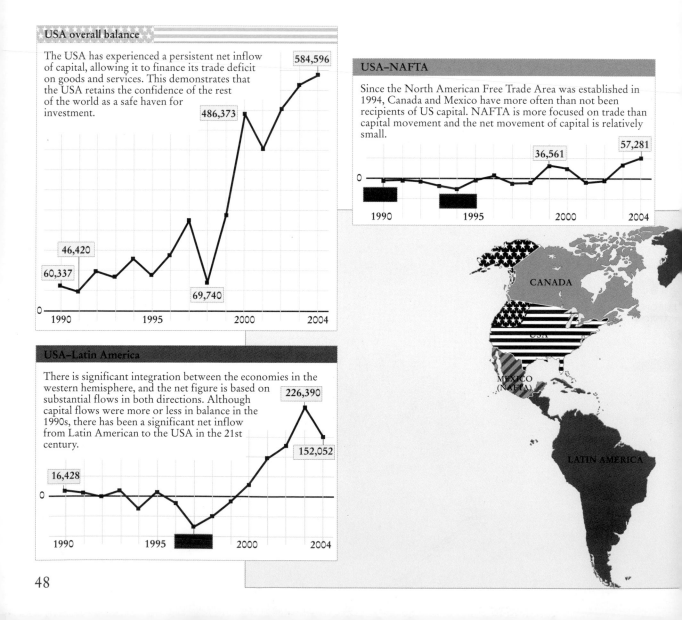

USA overall balance

The USA has experienced a persistent net inflow of capital, allowing it to finance its trade deficit on goods and services. This demonstrates that the USA retains the confidence of the rest of the world as a safe haven for investment.

584,596

486,373

46,420

60,337

69,740

1990   1995   2000   2004

USA–NAFTA

Since the North American Free Trade Area was established in 1994, Canada and Mexico have more often than not been recipients of US capital. NAFTA is more focused on trade than capital movement and the net movement of capital is relatively small.

0

36,561

57,281

1990   1995   2000   2004

CANADA

USA

MEXICO (NAFTA)

LATIN AMERICA

USA–Latin America

There is significant integration between the economies in the western hemisphere, and the net figure is based on substantial flows in both directions. Although capital flows were more or less in balance in the 1990s, there has been a significant net inflow from Latin American to the USA in the 21st century.

226,390

152,052

16,428

0

1990   1995   2000   2004

repatriated or reinvested. This requires a stable political and legal framework that is sympathetic to the market economy. The USA is the guarantor of this form of stability, and no other power is remotely capable of playing this role. Its success in overcoming the obstacles to freedom of capital, and in creating a single, global capital market since the end of the Cold War has been remarkable. America's indispensability in this respect is of much more significance than its economic vulnerability, and is the basis for its power and assertiveness in today's world.

NET FINANCIAL FLOW OF ASSETS

US-owned overseas assets balanced against
foreign-owned assets in the USA*
1990–2004
US$ millions

*including the purchase of Treasury and other government securities and foreign direct investment

——— net inflow

——— net outflow

USA–European Union

The flows of capital between the US and EU are twice as large as those for Japan or China, reflecting the major economic relationship between the two richest economic blocs in the world.

280,724

53,532

55,704

0

1990   1995   2000   2004

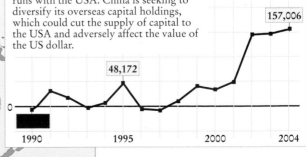

USA–Japan

Japan is the largest holder of US Treasury bonds, having built up its capital holding over many years of substantial trading surplus with the USA. The net inflow of capital from Japan to the USA reached almost 30% of the total in 2004, despite the slow growth of the Japanese economy over this period.

174,052

0

1990   1995   2000   2004

USA–Asia and Africa

The substantial increase in net inflow of capital from this region primarily reflects the growth of China, and the trade surplus it runs with the USA. China is seeking to diversify its overseas capital holdings, which could cut the supply of capital to the USA and adversely affect the value of the US dollar.

157,006

48,172

0

1990   1995   2000   2004

EUROPEAN
UNION

JAPAN

ASIA

AFRICA

THE DOLLAR

The power of the US dollar makes America the world's banker, with all the advantages that brings.

The role of the US dollar as a reserve currency has been an important source of American power. It was established as such after World War II, and its value was set at $35 dollars per ounce of gold. Other countries used it to conduct their international transactions, including settling their trade debts. Without it the rapid increase in trade that underpinned post-war prosperity would not have occurred.

The USA was providing a service to the world economy. However, unlike other countries, it was also able to use its own currency to settle its debts, and could do so simply by printing more dollars. Because of this, the USA was able to use dollars to finance its international activity without cost to its domestic economy, and the standard of living of US consumers was, in effect, subsidized. Of course, other countries were only willing to accept the dollar because of the dominant position of the USA in the world, and their confidence in the enduring value of the currency. The use of the dollar as a reserve currency was a form of "imperial rent" that allowed the USA to operate according to different economic rules from all other countries.

By 1971 the USA had printed so many dollars and put them into circulation in the world economy that other countries lost confidence in the convertibility of the dollar into gold at the fixed price, and

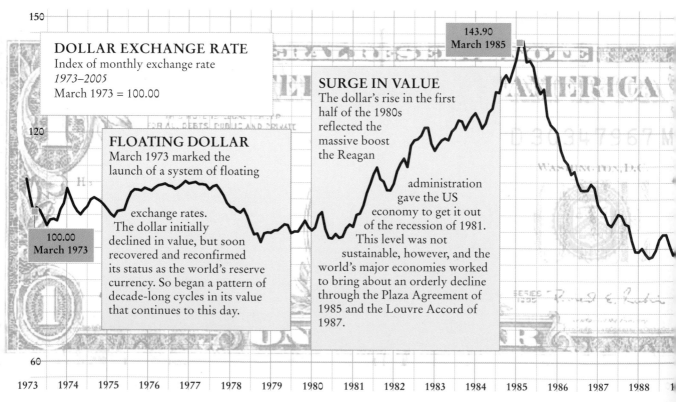

DOLLAR EXCHANGE RATE
Index of monthly exchange rate
1973–2005
March 1973 = 100.00

100.00
March 1973

FLOATING DOLLAR
March 1973 marked the launch of a system of floating exchange rates. The dollar initially declined in value, but soon recovered and reconfirmed its status as the world's reserve currency. So began a pattern of decade-long cycles in its value that continues to this day.

143.90
March 1985

SURGE IN VALUE
The dollar's rise in the first half of the 1980s reflected the massive boost the Reagan administration gave the US economy to get it out of the recession of 1981. This level was not sustainable, however, and the world's major economies worked to bring about an orderly decline through the Plaza Agreement of 1985 and the Louvre Accord of 1987.

1973 1974 1975 1976 1977 1978 1979 1980 1981 1982 1983 1984 1985 1986 1987 1988 1

became reluctant to use it. In 1971 President Nixon ended its fixed value in relation to gold, and by 1973 it, along with other major currencies, had adopted a system of flexible exchange rates.

From that point on the US dollar's strength has reflected, at least in part, the state of America's trade balance, and the country's relative economic strength. The value of the dollar against the currencies of its trading partners has therefore varied considerably. The international use of the dollar declined somewhat in the 1970s and 1980s, but it has grown since the 1990s, and in 2004 two-thirds of official foreign exchange reserves worldwide were held in dollars.

This means that, although the USA can no longer simply print its way out of economic trouble, its reserve role remains strong. Other countries, by holding their reserves in dollars and investing in US Treasury bonds, not only express their continuing confidence in the USA as a stable repository of value, but develop an interest in maintaining US prosperity.

The dollar is now uniquely well-placed to benefit from the defining development in the global economy – the growth of emerging markets – because a very large proportion of international reserve holdings and cross-border transactions in Latin America and Asia are in dollars.

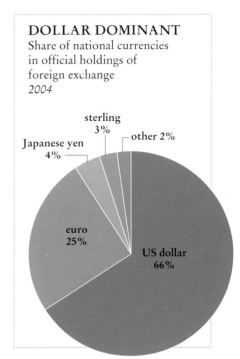

DOLLAR DOMINANT
Share of national currencies in official holdings of foreign exchange
2004

- sterling 3%
- other 2%
- Japanese yen 4%
- euro 25%
- US dollar 66%

LOSS OF CONFIDENCE
Domestic economic weakness drove the dollar down, but the low point it reached in March 1995 was triggered by the Clinton administration's bailout of the Mexican peso, during which America's reserves were used up. This undermined investor confidence, and triggered a run on the dollar.

CONCERN ABOUT THE DEFICIT
The growing US deficits in international trade and domestic public spending have generated concern about the long-term health of the US economy. The dollar remains the pre-eminent international currency, and this recent decline repeats the cycle of the past 30 years, but the reduced international demand for dollars, as investors turn to the euro and other currencies, may make recovery from the current low point more difficult than in earlier cycles.

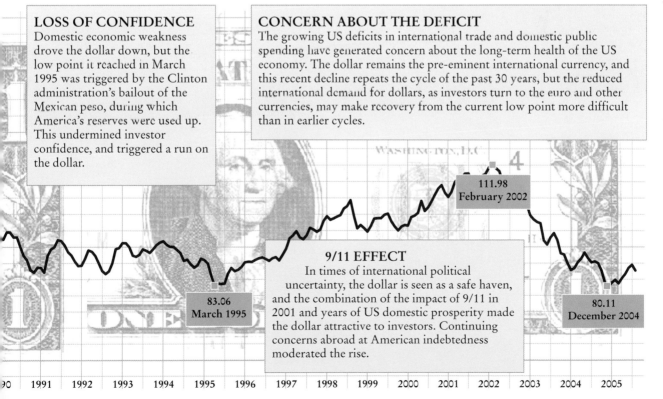

111.98
February 2002

9/11 EFFECT
In times of international political uncertainty, the dollar is seen as a safe haven, and the combination of the impact of 9/11 in 2001 and years of US domestic prosperity made the dollar attractive to investors. Continuing concerns abroad at American indebtedness moderated the rise.

83.06
March 1995

80.11
December 2004

90 | 1991 | 1992 | 1993 | 1994 | 1995 | 1996 | 1997 | 1998 | 1999 | 2000 | 2001 | 2002 | 2003 | 2004 | 2005

Chapter Four

PEOPLE

The age of globalization has seen the movement of trade and capital around the world increase dramatically, in terms of both speed and volume. It has also impacted on the daily lives of people, generating a quantum leap in mobility.

The USA occupies a dual role in migration. It has taken the lead in creating the global market, thereby establishing human mobility as a major means of economic betterment. However, this process is not smooth, and the new world order has been beset by political crises that have caused mass misery, hardship and displacement. Global migration patterns reflect the human consequences of the politics and the economics of American-driven global reorganization.

The USA does not stand apart from these global trends, but is being transformed by them. We are witnessing one of the major periods of immigration in US history. Today's migrants are more diverse in origin than before, and immigration is becoming truly global. In 2005, the USA received migrants from 200 countries, and its make-up increasingly reflects America's conception of itself as a universal society.

Increased mobility brings new groups into contact with each other, and challenges the existing social order. As American society becomes more diverse and multicultural, people have to find new ways of living together. When this takes place in conditions of inequality, as it normally does, the challenge is all the greater. The USA is the prime mover behind this trend but also, because of its history as an immigrant society, the prime exemplar of how to cope with these problems. If its imperial foreign policy creates problems of social cohesion across the world, its domestic flexibility may provide guidance on how to cope effectively with them.

Reconciling the need for labor to feed expanding economies with the often tense social consequences of migration is a major challenge of the age. More than any other area, it tests America's claim to be a universal nation, and reveals it to be one whose traditionally open and welcoming character is now under severe pressure, and whose responsibility for solutions that make the daily lives of real people more bearable is immense.

> " MIGRATION IS ONE OF THE MAJOR TIES THAT BIND OUR SOCIETIES. "
>
> PRESIDENT GEORGE W. BUSH
> FEBRUARY 16, 2001

Immigration

There has been a dramatic change in the pattern of immigration to the USA since 1965.

In 2005, the number of immigrants in the USA exceeded 38 million – 13 percent of the population. If the upwards trend continues, by 2010 the proportion of "foreign-born stock" will surpass 15 percent. Migrants are entering from over 200 countries – a much wider range than in previous periods – and this new pattern of immigration is massively impacting on the ethnic composition of American society.

The largest source of immigrants is the Americas, with Asia running a close second. In 2005, there were over 3.5 million Chinese, 2.5 million Filipino, and 2.5 million Indian, Americans. There were also 1.2 million people of Vietnamese descent, as a result of the Vietnam War, and 3.5 million Arab Americans, including 300,000 Iraqis.

Immigrants generate economic dynamism, providing a source of cheap labor in service and manufacturing industries, keeping wages, and therefore inflation, in check. Increasingly, they also provide scarce skills for the advanced service sectors, and have helped the American economy to grow faster than other advanced economies.

The economic benefits of immigration lie behind America's historic character as a relatively open and welcoming society. But as migration reaches new heights, accepted social patterns are being challenged, and America is becoming more like other Western countries, adopting a suspicious, closed mentality that sees immigrants as a threat. Social tension has increased as many Americans feel that immigrants are taking their jobs, and taking advantage of welfare payments. Immigrant groups are also competing among themselves, and with African Americans, to fight their way up from the bottom of the social pile.

There has been much speculation as to whether these changes will re-orient US foreign policy away from Europe, towards Asia, Latin America and even Africa. There is little evidence of this, however, or of an understanding of the problems of the less-developed regions, and the main impact remains on the dynamics of US society itself.

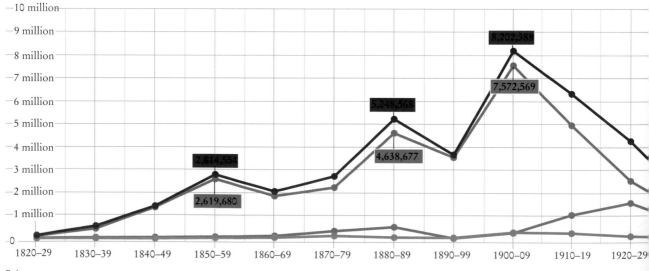

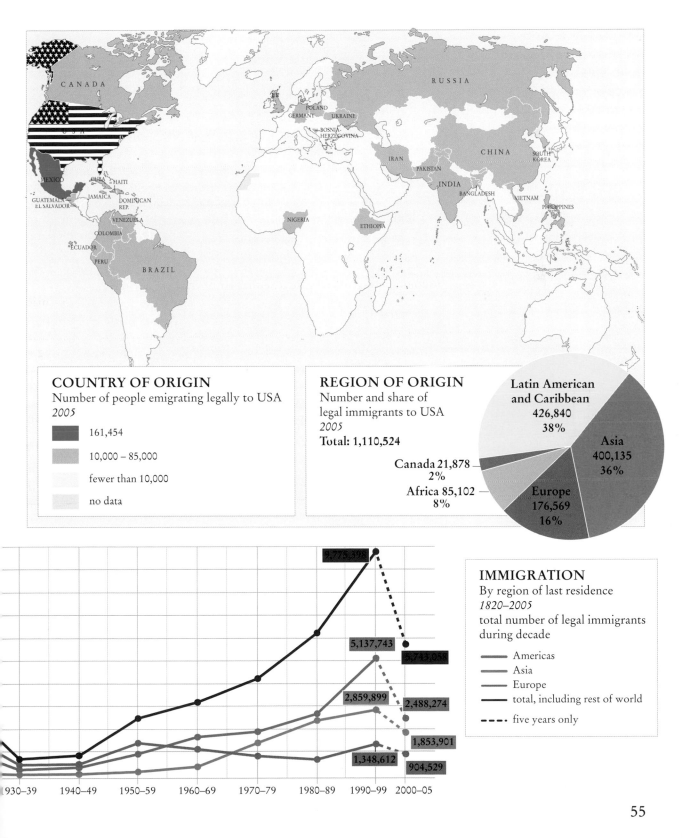

COUNTRY OF ORIGIN

Number of people emigrating legally to USA
2005

- 161,454
- 10,000 – 85,000
- fewer than 10,000
- no data

REGION OF ORIGIN

Number and share of
legal immigrants to USA
2005
Total: 1,110,524

Canada 21,878
2%

Africa 85,102
8%

Latin American
and Caribbean
426,840
38%

Asia
400,135
36%

Europe
176,569
16%

IMMIGRATION

By region of last residence
1820–2005
total number of legal immigrants
during decade

—— Americas
—— Asia
—— Europe
—— total, including rest of world
----- five years only

2,775,398

5,137,743

5,743,058

2,859,899

2,488,274

1,853,901

1,348,612

904,529

1930–39   1940–49   1950–59   1960–69   1970–79   1980–89   1990–99   2000–05

55

US domination of its hemisphere is being transformed by mass migration of Latin Americans into the USA.

Most Latin Americans have seen the "Yanquis" as an imperial presence throughout their modern history. Since the Cold War, the USA has imposed a market economy on the region, dominating it through the "natural" mechanisms of the market. The major initiative to promote economic integration has been the North America Free Trade Area (NAFTA). There have been ambitions for a free-trade area to cover the whole of the Americas, but this has been resisted by several South American states, which have set up their own free-trade organization, MERCOSUR.

Formal initiatives have been less important than US domination of the movement of capital, and the increased movement of people. Capital flows south from the USA to take advantage of cheap labor, and people flow north to meet the demand for the same. Hispanics have made up nearly half of all immigrants since 1968. Although they are still concentrated disproportionately in the southern heartlands, they are spreading across the country, and now make up at least 10 percent of the population in over a quarter of US states.

The scale of recent immigration has led to a major political debate in which harsh measures, such as the construction of a border fence and the repatriation of illegal migrants, are called for in Congress. This is balanced by an increasingly powerful Hispanic political voice. The debate reflects an ambivalent attitude among whites, with concern about the job losses, crime, and welfare problems they associate with immigrants weighed against a respect for the strong family values evident in the Hispanic community, and recognition of the contribution of Hispanics to the economy.

These currents of opinion create political dilemmas for the government, but, more important, they demonstrate that the great influx of Hispanics is changing the social fabric of American society. Over 10 percent of Americans now speak Spanish at home, and the refusal of many whites to accept immigration is mirrored by the resistance of many Hispanics to the idea of integration. Anglo and Hispanic America have a common destiny, however – one that will be shaped by whether white America maintains its imperial pretension and seeks the path of repression in response to these challenges, or reasserts the openness and flexibility that is the best of America's immigrant heritage.

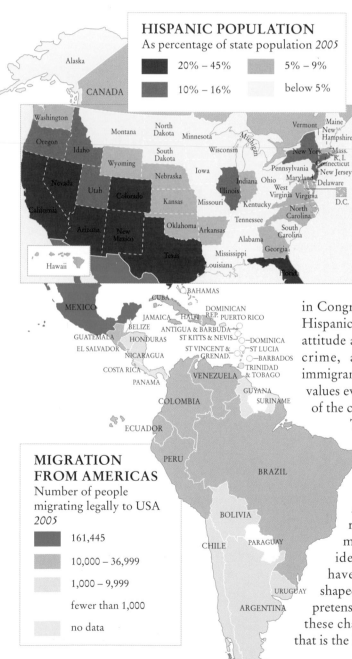

HISPANIC POPULATION
As percentage of state population *2005*

- 20% – 45%
- 10% – 16%
- 5% – 9%
- below 5%

MIGRATION FROM AMERICAS
Number of people migrating legally to USA *2005*

- 161,445
- 10,000 – 36,999
- 1,000 – 9,999
- fewer than 1,000
- no data

ILLEGAL IMMIGRATION

The number of illegal immigrants in the USA is unclear, but a consensus estimate is around 11 million. Mexicans make up over 50 percent of illegal immigrants, and since 1995 illegal Mexican immigrants have outnumbered the legal.

Illegal immigrants work primarily in agriculture, construction, domestic service, and food preparation, and are more poorly paid than their legal counterparts. Thus, they bolster US corporate profit and help to reduce the cost of the comfortable lifestyle enjoyed by America's middle classes. The living and working conditions of illegal migrants exposes the brutal underbelly of American society, which imports into the heart of the wealthiest country in the world the kind of poverty that is so familiar in developing countries, and demonstrates that imperial exploitation is no respecter of borders.

But even as they benefit from this "subsidy" many Americans express a fear of illegal immigration, which has led to firmer policing of the southern US border. Such is the demand for cheap labor that the effect of border controls and other restrictions is not to stop illegal immigration, but to criminalize immigrants, keeping them tied to an underground economy, and giving licence to local repressive measures and vigilantism.

INCREASE IN ILLEGALS
Number estimated to have entered USA in each 5-year period
1980–2005

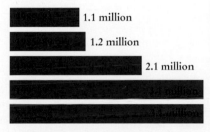

	1.1 million
	1.2 million
	2.1 million

ILLEGALS
Major populations by state
2005

2.8m	California
1.4m	Texas
0.85m	Florida
0.56m	New York
0.52m	Illinois
0.48m	Arizona
0.47m	Georgia
0.38m	New Jersey
0.36m	North Carolina
0.24m	Nevada

CUBA

There are 1.5 million Cuban Americans. Two-thirds live in Florida, and are richer, more educated, older, more likely to vote Republican, than other Hispanic groups.

Since the 1959 revolution, Cubans have migrated to the USA in waves. First, wealthy Cubans fled from the Castro regime, followed by an orderly, government-sanctioned departure of middle-class Cubans. In 1980, Castro allowed a free exodus from the port of Mariel, but in recent years there has been a quota system, supplemented by an intermittent influx of rafters, who are given asylum if they reach the US shore. Cuban migrants have received a warmer welcome than other Hispanics, as they are seen as refugees from tyranny.

Cuba represents an affront to America's presumed dominance in its backyard, and successive US administrations have tried to overturn its regime. Continuing migration, and, in particular, the expulsion from Cuba of people from prisons and mental institutions during the Mariel episode, demonstrate that insulation from the consequences of foreign policy is impossible. Cuba literally brings home to Americans that regime change is a dangerous game.

CUBAN MIGRANTS
Number estimated to have entered USA in each 10-year period
1951–2000

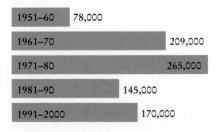

1951–60	78,000
1961–70	209,000
1971–80	265,000
1981–90	145,000
1991–2000	170,000

ECONOMIC MIGRATION

More people are living outside their country of birth than ever before, leading to a tighter integration of rich and poor countries.

Globalization has led to a massive worldwide movement of people, with at least 3 percent of the world's population now living outside their country of birth. This mass migration is driven by the inequality between nations; people from poor countries who are seeking out an income for their families are drawn towards richer countries hungry for cheap labor. Industrialization is also causing a movement from rural to urban environments, often resulting in areas of mass poverty surrounding the new megacities of the developing world.

Migration is integral to international capitalism, in which America is the dominant force. The USA accounts for one-fifth of the world's migrants, with a net annual influx of over 1 million legal migrants. As much as one-fifth of global migration is unauthorized, and the USA also has the largest number of illegal migrants – approximately one-third of the world total. Migration plays a key role in America's economic success. Migrants not only perform jobs at the bottom of the economic scale – dirty, demeaning, difficult, and dangerous jobs that Americans do not want – but provide a regular infusion of skilled labor, even though this drains talent from countries least able to afford it.

The flow is not all one way, however. Many jobs formerly located in the USA have moved to developing countries through outsourcing or tax-free border zones. This process is spreading from manufacturing to service industries, such at ICT, where labor costs can be reduced by up to 90 percent.

Economic migration has become critical to the health of some developing economies, but it revitalizes rich countries, in particular the USA.

LARGEST MIGRANT POPULATIONS
by host country
2005 millions

38.4	USA
12.1	Russia
10.1	Germany
6.8	Ukraine
6.5	France
6.4	Saudi Arabia
6.1	Canada
5.7	India
5.4	UK
4.8	Spain
4.1	Australia
	3.3 Pakistan

GLOBAL MIGRATION
Average annual net gain or loss of people
2000–05
by region

Net gain

	1.3 million or more
	600,000
	356,000
	1 – 250,000

Net loss

	1 – 250,000
	294,000 – 475,000
	878,000

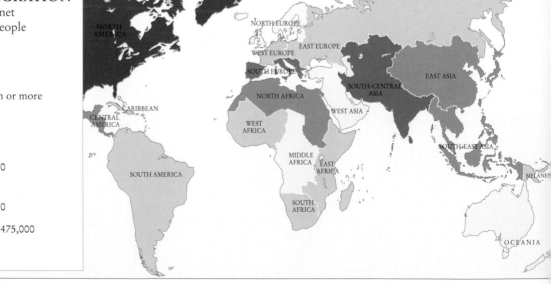

FEMINIZATION OF MIGRATION

The number of female migrants worldwide doubled between 1985 and 2005. At almost 100 million, it now exceeds the number of males. Domestic and sex work predominate – sectors generally unregulated by effective labor laws, making women migrants susceptible to exploitation. Half a million women are sex trafficked across borders each year in a manifestation of the dark underside of globalization.

The majority of migrants to the USA are female. Migration can emancipate women, giving them financial independence that enhances their status at home. Some female migrants are highly skilled; a quarter of US urban nurses are foreign born, for example. But forced migration is equally characteristic: 15,000 women are trafficked to the USA each year, from 50 countries, to work in sweatshops, brothels, bars, farm camps, and in domestic service.

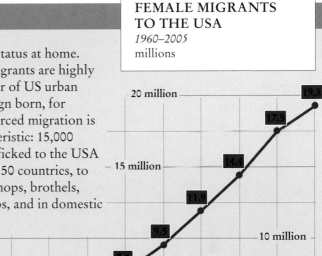

FEMALE MIGRANTS TO THE USA
1960–2005
millions

FINANCIAL REMITTANCES

The possibility of earning money to send to their families back home is what motivates most migrants to seek employment abroad. Remittances to developing economies now exceed $150 billion a year – three times the amount provided by official development assistance, and second only to foreign direct investment (FDI) as a source of funding for developing countries.

Remittances are a mirror image of international migration: people move in one direction, money flows in the other. Latin America receives around three-quarters of its remittances from the USA, with more than 12 million Latinos remitting $45 billion a year in 2006, an increase of 50 percent in two years.

This transnational economic network has become an essential characteristic of many developing economies and is key to their viability. More than 20 countries receive remittances that exceed 10 percent of their GDP. The problem is that remittances create dependency, especially when they are used for immediate consumption rather than for investment in self-sustaining

growth. As a result, developing countries become vulnerable to policies that affect this lifeline, giving the USA and other rich countries a tight grip on the world economy.

LATIN AMERICAN REMITTANCES
Total received by country *2004*
US$ millions

- over $18,000
- $1,000 – $4,000
- $100 – $999
- $1 – $99

POLITICAL REFUGEES

American influence in political upheaval and conflicts has contributed to the displacement of millions of people.

There are officially over 20 million people "of concern" to the Office of the United Nations High Commissioner for Refugees (UNHCR). This includes people who have fled their own country into another, those who have been displaced within their own country, asylum-seekers and stateless persons. It does not include economic migrants, or unofficial flows of migrants.

People are primarily driven from their homes by conflict, which is often the result of political failure. Although not exclusively the product of US policies, the pattern of displacement does reveal massive American influence. The USA may be one of the largest receivers of asylum seekers, and grant citizenship to more people than any other country in response to humanitarian crises, but the mass misery behind these figures bears the mark of conflicts in which it has been involved in some capacity.

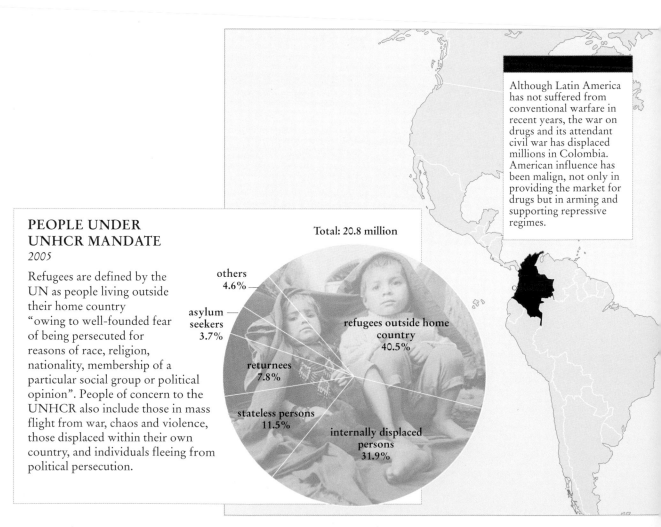

Although Latin America has not suffered from conventional warfare in recent years, the war on drugs and its attendant civil war has displaced millions in Colombia. American influence has been malign, not only in providing the market for drugs but in arming and supporting repressive regimes.

PEOPLE UNDER UNHCR MANDATE
2005

Refugees are defined by the UN as people living outside their home country "owing to well-founded fear of being persecuted for reasons of race, religion, nationality, membership of a particular social group or political opinion". People of concern to the UNHCR also include those in mass flight from war, chaos and violence, those displaced within their own country, and individuals fleeing from political persecution.

Total: 20.8 million

others 4.6%

asylum seekers 3.7%

returnees 7.8%

stateless persons 11.5%

refugees outside home country 40.5%

internally displaced persons 31.9%

60

The greatest impact comes from the War on Terror that the USA has been waging since September 2001, but the pattern of displaced people also reflects realignments and conflicts, particularly ethnic, arising from the new world order that the USA has established since the end of the Cold War.

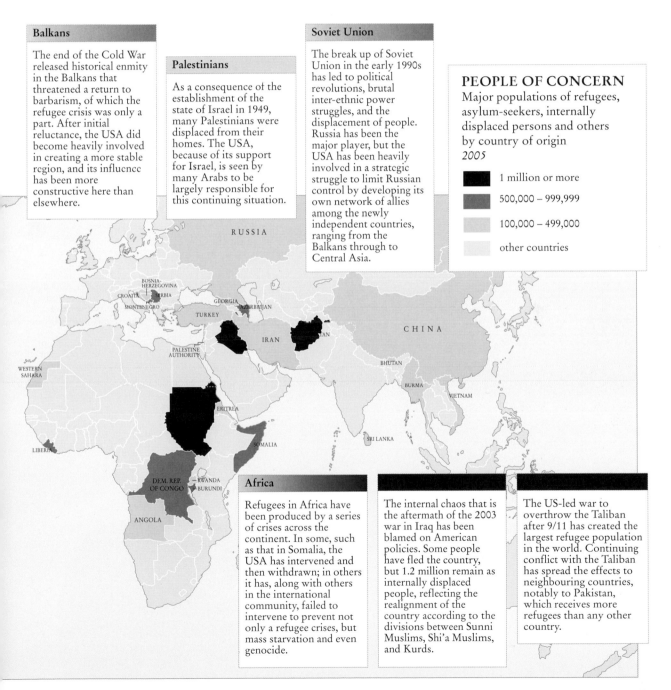

Balkans

The end of the Cold War released historical enmity in the Balkans that threatened a return to barbarism, of which the refugee crisis was only a part. After initial reluctance, the USA did become heavily involved in creating a more stable region, and its influence has been more constructive here than elsewhere.

Palestinians

As a consequence of the establishment of the state of Israel in 1949, many Palestinians were displaced from their homes. The USA, because of its support for Israel, is seen by many Arabs to be largely responsible for this continuing situation.

Soviet Union

The break up of Soviet Union in the early 1990s has led to political revolutions, brutal inter-ethnic power struggles, and the displacement of people. Russia has been the major player, but the USA has been heavily involved in a strategic struggle to limit Russian control by developing its own network of allies among the newly independent countries, ranging from the Balkans through to Central Asia.

PEOPLE OF CONCERN

Major populations of refugees, asylum-seekers, internally displaced persons and others by country of origin
2005

- 1 million or more
- 500,000 – 999,999
- 100,000 – 499,000
- other countries

Africa

Refugees in Africa have been produced by a series of crises across the continent. In some, such as that in Somalia, the USA has intervened and then withdrawn; in others it has, along with others in the international community, failed to intervene to prevent not only a refugee crises, but mass starvation and even genocide.

The internal chaos that is the aftermath of the 2003 war in Iraq has been blamed on American policies. Some people have fled the country, but 1.2 million remain as internally displaced people, reflecting the realignment of the country according to the divisions between Sunni Muslims, Shi'a Muslims, and Kurds.

The US-led war to overthrow the Taliban after 9/11 has created the largest refugee population in the world. Continuing conflict with the Taliban has spread the effects to neighbouring countries, notably to Pakistan, which receives more refugees than any other country.

Chapter Five
MILITARY

The end of the Cold War in the 1990s engendered an era of international uncertainty, instability and armed conflict, and the role of the USA in maintaining political order is as vital as its role in maintaining a stable market system. In addition, the USA has its own agenda and national interests to pursue, and it is its capacity to mobilize its armed forces, rather than its economic strength, that is the bedrock of its imperial power.

In order to maintain this power, the US military budget dwarfs that of any other nation or combination of nations. America fully intends to maintain spending at levels that will preclude any nation, or combination of nations, challenging its military supremacy.

This investment in the military not only affects the rest of the world, it also determines the internal character of American society. Economic growth relies on high levels of military spending, with millions of jobs dependent on the arms industry and defense expenditure. A country that before World War II maintained only a small standing army has been transformed into a militaristic culture. As a result, political fighting for the division of the spoils of arms contracts has become one of the main axes of US politics. The internal interests within the USA that depend on military expenditure make it difficult to cut spending, and this is one of the drivers behind the US creation and exaggeration of threats to its security.

The USA projects its force in many ways, most obviously through a vast network of bases, supplemented by agreements with other governments that give it military access to facilities in times of crisis. These agreements are predicated on friendly governments being willing to host a US presence. Such is the attractiveness of good relations with the superpower, that other states are often willing to do this at the expense of their own domestic popularity. The imperial largesse the USA can deploy to underpin friendly relations can take many forms of support and inducements, including arms sales financed by aid. When inducements fail, direct or covert intervention to install client regimes is another option. The power of the panoply of weapons in America's arsenal is a mechanism for creating dependency around the world, and a critical element of the creation of Pax Americana.

> " WE MUST DETER AND DEFEND AGAINST THE THREAT BEFORE IT IS UNLEASHED. "
>
> US NATIONAL SECURITY STRATEGY 2002

MILITARY SPENDING

US military spending has fluctuated in response to perceived threats and presidential ambitions for world domination.

The growth of military spending by the USA since the turn of the century is projected to continue, because higher spending is needed to transform the US armed forces into a new, more flexible and mobile configuration, suited to meeting the threats of the 21st century.

In recent years, official figures underestimate actual spending because they cover only peacetime manning and support operations.

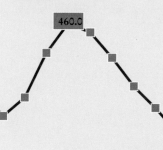

1945–55

The boost to economic activity given by military spending during World War II came to an abrupt end in 1947, causing fears that the USA would return to the depression of the 1930s. The declaration of a Cold War with communism in the late 1940s provided a rationale for increased spending and this was enhanced by American involvement in the Korean War, which led military spending to quadruple from its immediate post-war low point.

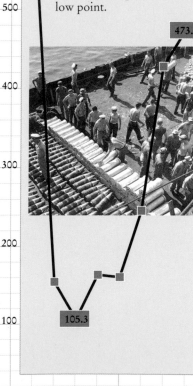

1955–65

After the peak caused by the Korean conflict, spending remained fairly constant for the next decade. Even though a rather tired Eisenhower presidency was replaced by the more dynamic and aggressive Kennedy administration, the security strategy remained unchanged.

The focus on nuclear weapons produced the so-called doctrine of "Mutual Assured Destruction". This was relied on at the expense of an emphasis on building up conventional arms in the fight against communism. It was a strategy shared by Eisenhower and Kennedy, and accounts for the constancy of spending.

1965–75

Expenditure again rose significantly because of the need to finance expanding American involvement in the war in Vietnam.

Military spending went beyond levels necessary to maintain economic growth and led to spending being diverted from social programs. The economy overheated and inflation rose. After reaching its peak at the turn of the decade, spending declined slowly as American involvement in Vietnam wound down and a policy of détente with the Soviet Union was pursued.

US$ billion

600 | 612.7
473.7
500
460.0
365.7
400
277.1
300
200
105.3
100

1946   1950   1955   1960   1965   1970

Since 2003, the Iraq war has cost an additional $220 billion, and for the fiscal year 2008 the administration of George W. Bush has requested from Congress a further appropriation of $141 billion to cover the costs of the wars in Iraq and Afghanistan.

In real terms, spending is now approaching its highest level since the end of World War II. Continued increases will be harder to achieve in the face of a large federal deficit and competing domestic demands.

US MILITARY SPENDING
Annual expenditure
1946–2006
constant 2003 US$ billions

1995–2005
Spending continued to reflect the post-Cold War peace dividend for the rest of the 1990s, and there was a further moderate decline in Clinton's second term. Rather, as when Reagan took over from Carter, George W. Bush came to office promising to reverse the trend under Clinton and to reassert US military pre-eminence. Planned rises in spending were accelerated beyond expectations after September 11, 2001, and, in the first half of the decade, experienced another 30-percent surge similar to that of the 1980s.

1975–85
In the immediate post-Vietnam era under President Carter, expenditure remained constant, as the foreign policy emphasis moved away from military confrontation, leading to charges that military spending was too low to maintain America's position as the number one world power.

1985–95
High levels of spending were maintained in Reagan's second term, reaching their highest ever levels at the end of the 1980s. This coincided with the end of the Cold War.

This was President Reagan's message when he won election in1980 and he acted upon it, authorizing a massive increase in military spending of over 30 percent in the first half of the 1980s, and accompanying it with a much more strident foreign policy towards the Soviet Union.

Reagan's supporters argued that victory the collapse of communism was due to the inability of the Soviet Union to compete with the USA in the arms race. After the Cold War, spending levels declined gradually, despite the costs of the first Gulf War, as President Clinton again shifted foreign policy priorities away from military dominance.

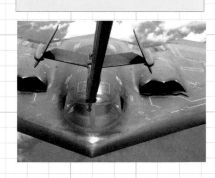

437.4

304.8

399.4

3.0

1980   1985   1990   1995   2000   2005 2006

COMPARATIVE MILITARY SPENDING

Total US military spending is greater than that of the next five largest spenders combined, giving the USA a military strength beyond that of any other state.

The military spending of the USA is five times greater than that of the next largest spender, China, and dwarfs that of all other countries. The size of its military budget gives it a pre-eminence in this field that is even greater than its domination of world markets. It also gives the USA a military profile that is qualitatively different from that of any other state.

While this level of expenditure is reflected in a high spend per person, it represents only 3.3 percent of the US National Income. This is exceeded by many other countries, primarily those in areas where there is an imminent threat of conflict or a chronic security problem, such as the Middle East, parts of Africa, Greece and Turkey, the Balkans, the Caspian and the Indian sub-continent.

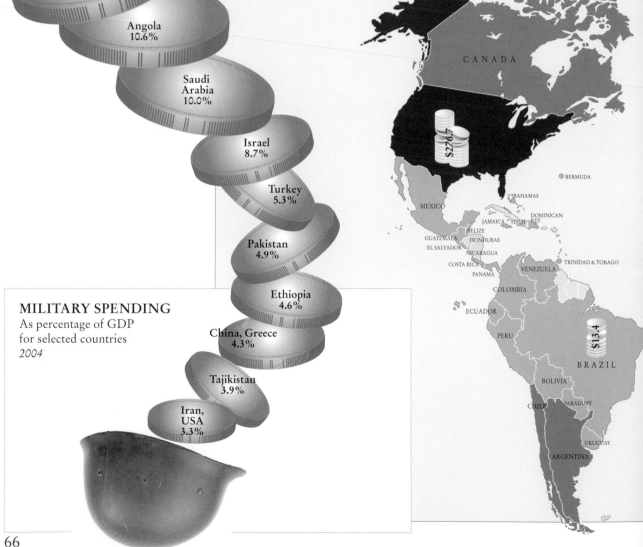

Jordan 14.6%
Angola 10.6%
Saudi Arabia 10.0%
Israel 8.7%
Turkey 5.3%
Pakistan 4.9%
Ethiopia 4.6%
China, Greece 4.3%
Tajikistan 3.9%
Iran, USA 3.3%

MILITARY SPENDING
As percentage of GDP for selected countries
2004

US military pre-eminence enables it to project force beyond its borders in a way no other country is able to do. The USA can engage in more than one major conflict at a time, and has a range and sophistication of weaponry that makes it unchallengeable in conventional military terms. While other countries have nuclear weapons and new weapons of mass destruction, none has more than regional military capability. The European Union is the only possible exception, but it is neither sufficiently cohesive nor independent to exercise its combined military might.

Since the disintegration of the Soviet Union in the early 1990s, the USA faces no competitor with a global military capability and is unlikely to do so in the foreseeable future.

MILITARY SPENDING
per person
2004
US$

$500 and above

$100 – $499

$10 - $99

below $10

no data

Total military spending
2004

above $275 billion
value given

$10 – 56 billion
value given

MILITARY AT HOME

Military spending boosts local economies. Defense spending, and thus foreign policy, is therefore partly driven by domestic political pressures.

Three quarters of the US Defense Department budget is spent at home – on payroll, procurement contracts, pensions, and on the military bases that are spread throughout the country. In 2003, this amounted to $320 billion – an increase of 50 percent since the mid-1990s.

This total military spend averages out at more than $1,000 per person in the USA; in some states the average exceeds $3,000. It represents a massive financial injection into virtually every local economy in the country.

While the distribution of these funds is in part determined by military considerations – naval bases usually have to be on the coast – the process of allocating defense spending is hugely political, and the pattern of spending reflects the balance of political power as much as the security needs of the USA. It is an open secret that one of the main tasks of all legislators who are sent to Washington is to make sure that their state or district receives a fair share of this federal largesse.

Legislators compete fiercely with one another to win projects for their constituency, but they are linked by a common interest: keeping their constituents happy, and their own elected position secure, by maximizing the size of the overall spend. This creates a network of vested interests in the militarization of American society that informs the character of its foreign policy.

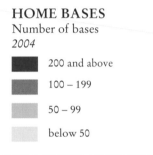

HOME BASES
Number of bases
2004

- 200 and above
- 100 – 199
- 50 – 99
- below 50

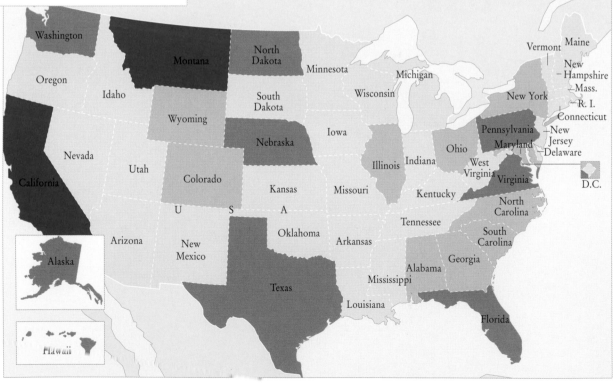

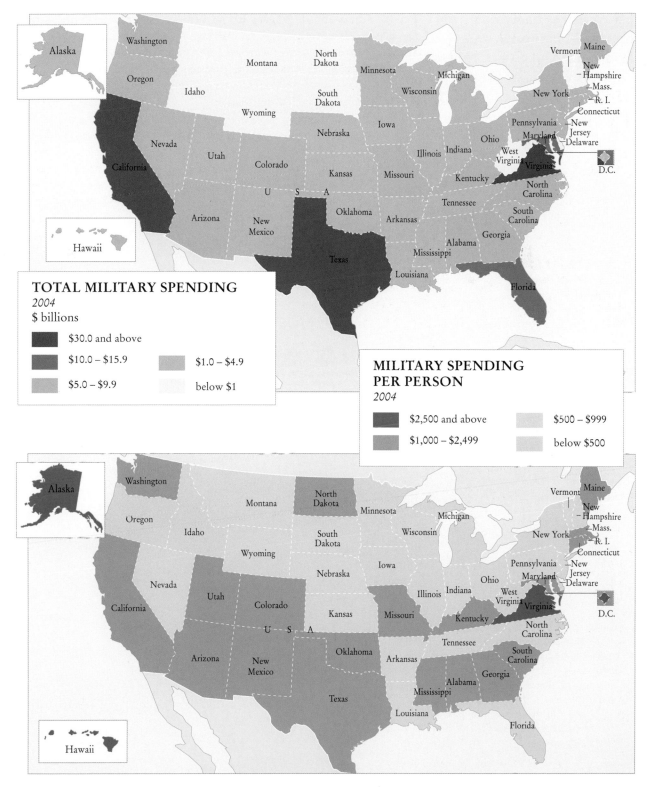

TOTAL MILITARY SPENDING
2004
$ billions

- $30.0 and above
- $10.0 – $15.9
- $5.0 – $9.9
- $1.0 – $4.9
- below $1

MILITARY SPENDING PER PERSON
2004

- $2,500 and above
- $1,000 – $2,499
- $500 – $999
- below $500

MILITARY ABROAD

US overseas bases and military personnel symbolize the power that defines American imperialism.

In 2006 there were nearly half a million US military personnel overseas. Exactly where troops are at any one time is not easy to ascertain, but the 85,000 in Europe, long after the collapse of the former Soviet Union, indicates that the distribution of troops and bases is something of a legacy of past wars and crises. Even when threats diminish, bases are hard to relinquish.

Change is underway, however. While military bases around the world are an essential symbol of America's superpower status, the importance of these bases is being increasingly seen, not in terms of personnel, but in terms of their potential for the deployment of weapons. Instead of large, permanent facilities, with extensive civilian and welfare support functions, the USA is now seeking to have smaller,

PEOPLE AND BASES

Number of US military
and support personnel
in foreign countries
and US overseas territories
2006

- 150,000 or more
- 10,000 – 64,000
- 1,000 – 3,500
- 100 – 999
- fewer than 100
- none

Number of bases
2006
number given

- 275
- 50 – 99
- below 50

The official figures for US bases given by the Defense Department omit bases in the Middle East and former Soviet Union, and exclude the massive "temporary" bases used for active operations, such as those supporting Operation Enduring Freedom in and around Afghanistan, and Operation Iraqi Freedom.

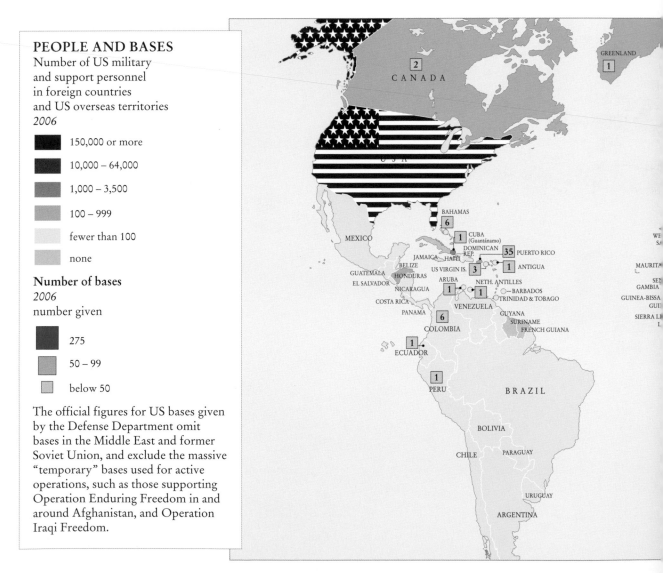

more flexible bases. These are often foreign-owned but with US access rights, which can be quickly activated when needed. With this revised approach, bases become lily pads – jumping off points for global operations.

When the new pattern is established, it will reflect obvious threats, such as that to oil supplies from the Middle East or the Caspian region for which new facilities around the Black Sea are already being created. It will also provide improved military projection into what the USA sees as the "Arc of Instability" – running from Latin America across the Horn of Africa to the sub-continent and South-East Asia. The USA will be able to intervene anywhere in the world, not only in response to, but in order to pre-empt, attacks from terrorists or hostile states.

Caspian region

The region contains potential long-term energy supplies that the USA is keen to protect against Russian and Chinese influence. Since 9/11 the region has also provided the facilities needed to support US troops in Afghanistan and to combat terrorist groups. This has been achieved by the USA making arrangements for amenable governments, such as that of Kyrgyzstan, to provide access to military facilities, without the necessity for a large US presence. This creates the impression of reducing the US military presence abroad while actually extending US influence and effective force projection.

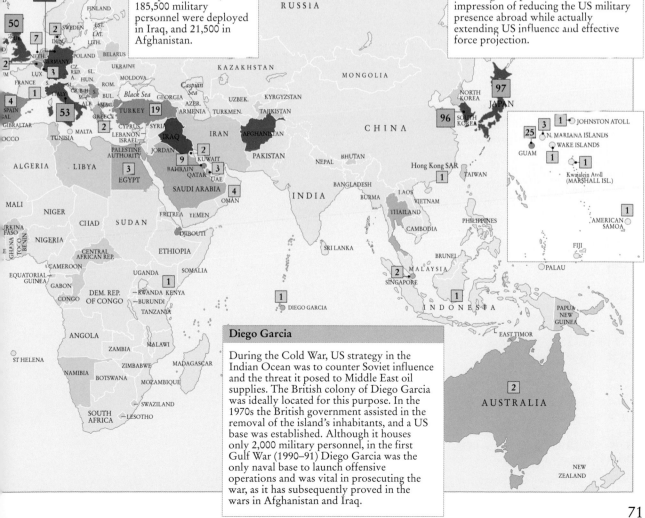

Troops deployed

In September 2006, 185,500 military personnel were deployed in Iraq, and 21,500 in Afghanistan.

Diego Garcia

During the Cold War, US strategy in the Indian Ocean was to counter Soviet influence and the threat it posed to Middle East oil supplies. The British colony of Diego Garcia was ideally located for this purpose. In the 1970s the British government assisted in the removal of the island's inhabitants, and a US base was established. Although it houses only 2,000 military personnel, in the first Gulf War (1990–91) Diego Garcia was the only naval base to launch offensive operations and was vital in prosecuting the war, as it has subsequently proved in the wars in Afghanistan and Iraq.

ARMS SALES

The USA is the world's largest arms exporter, and the US government manipulates this trade to influence world events.

The health of the US arms industry, and the economic well-being of many US localities, both depend on arms exports, and US arms manufacturers dominate the world trade. However, this trade neither operates in a free market, nor follows a democratic human rights agenda. The US government works closely with its arms industry to win contracts, and appears willing to sell arms to virtually any country, irrespective of their human rights record. This is because arms exports represent more than a source of profit; they are a vital element in US imperial strategy. Creating a dependency on their weapons gives the USA direct control of a client country's capacity to defend itself, or to wage aggression, and indirect control over its wider foreign policy.

Although other countries attempt to diversify their arms supplies to give themselves more autonomy, the USA's financial and technological pre-eminence, together with its ability to offer better terms through financing packages allied to its aid policy, makes arms sales a major source of its influence on world events. It is not unusual for the USA to

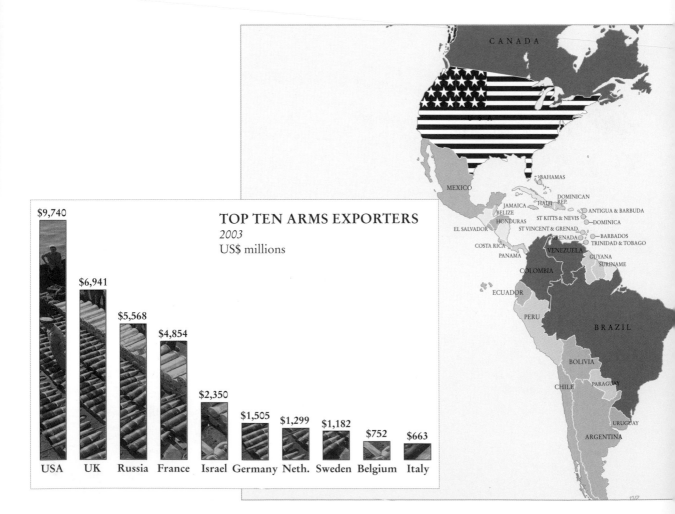

TOP TEN ARMS EXPORTERS
2003
US$ millions

$9,740	$6,941	$5,568	$4,854	$2,350	$1,505	$1,299	$1,182	$752	$663
USA	UK	Russia	France	Israel	Germany	Neth.	Sweden	Belgium	Italy

act as supplier to both sides in a potential conflict and to calibrate the weapons it sells so as to give itself leverage and the ability to manipulate the outcome of any conflict. This is evident in the arms it sells to Greece and Turkey, and a similar policy is developing on the Indian sub-continent as it sells ever-more sophisticated weapons to both India and Pakistan.

In the Middle East, the USA maintains Israeli military domination through arms sales and other forms of aid, but also has Saudi Arabia and Egypt, potential adversaries of Israel, as its biggest customers – although it never arms them to a level of sophistication that will threaten Israel. Similarly, in the Far East, where its influence over China is limited, the USA uses its arms sales to Taiwan as a sign of support, and as a way of restraining China militarily. When arms sales combine with US willingness to despatch naval carrier task forces to the Taiwan straits at the least sign of Chinese belligerence, this is America fulfilling its imperial role to maintain a peaceful status quo.

US ARMS SALES
Value of arms imported from USA
Oct 2001–Sept 2002
US$ millions

- $1,000 and above
- $100 – $999
- $10 – $99
- $1 – $9
- below $1
- no import or no data

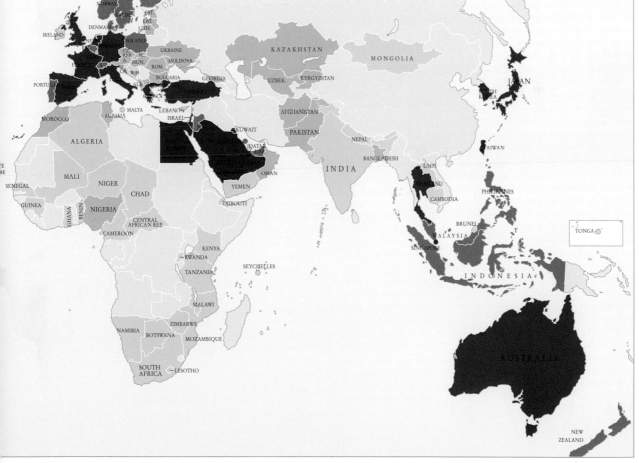

Chapter Six

NATIONAL SECURITY

During the Cold War, US security strategy was governed by the perceived need to contain communism, and intervention overseas was justified in these terms. Neo-Conservatives, who dominate the thinking of the Bush administration, argue that the aggressive anti-communist stance adopted by President Reagan in the 1980s not only won the Cold War, but left the USA as the only superpower, with an historically unique opportunity to dominate the new world order, by force if necessary. The Neo-Conservative perspective sees an activist foreign policy as not only protecting American interests, but as a way of fulfilling the USA's global responsibility to create a world based on American liberal principles. The alternative would be to cede the world to dictators, rogue states and terrorists who, in deadly combination, represent the new post-Cold War challenge to the US-inspired neo-liberal order.

The events of 9/11 crystallized the threat posed by this new challenge. In 2002 the USA revised its national security strategy, making clear its determination to defend itself against all threats. As long as there are terrorist groups willing to wreak havoc on the USA and its foreign interests, and countries willing to provide them with the means to do so, the USA's security strategy gives it license, indeed requires it, to use force. Although it claims to be acting only in self-defense against enemies that are the embodiment of evil and barbarism, America's response has in fact been aggressive and uncompromising, revealing more clearly than before its far-reaching, imperial ambition, and in the process forfeiting much of the sympathy it enjoyed in the immediate aftermath of the atrocity.

The factual record of US policy belies its defensive rationale, as is apparent from the consistent and extensive pattern of its intervention in the affairs of other countries since 1945. The contemporary threat from so-called rogue states is given more urgency by the possibility of their developing nuclear or other weapons of mass destruction. The connection to the justification given for the invasion of Iraq is clear.

> "
> WAR HAS BEEN WAGED
> AGAINST US BY STEALTH
> AND DECEIT AND MURDER...
> THE CONFLICT WAS BEGUN
> ON THE TIMING AND TERMS
> OF OTHERS. IT WILL END IN
> A WAY, AND AT AN HOUR,
> OF OUR CHOOSING. "
>
> PRESIDENT GEORGE W. BUSH
> THE NATIONAL CATHEDRAL
> WASHINGTON, D.C.
> SEPTEMBER 14, 2001

INTERVENTIONS: 1945–89

During the Cold War, the USA intervened in over 30 countries to prevent the spread of communism.

1948 1961
(Berlin)
GERMANY

YUGOSLAVIA
1946

1947–49 1967
GREECE

U S A

1965–66
DOMINICAN REP.

PUERTO RICO

1961 1962
CUBA

1950

1989

VIRGIN IS.

1983–89

1954 1966–67
GUATEMALA   HON.
EL SALVADOR

NICARAGUA

GRENADA
1983–84

1981–90

1981–92

1958 1964 1989–90
PANAMA

1964
BRAZIL

1986 BOLIVIA

1973
CHILE

1947
URUGUAY

Central America

The CIA intervened in Guatemala in 1954 to overthrow the legitimate government after it nationalized US company lands. A CIA-sponsored invasion of Cuba in 1961 was unsuccessful, but led to the 1962 Cuban Missile Crisis, which brought the world to the brink of nuclear war. Invasions of the Dominican Republic in 1965, Grenada in 1983 and Panama in 1989 illustrated the license the USA gave itself for overt intervention. This was complemented by indirect support the USA gave in the 1980s to repressive governments in El Salvador, Guatemala and to opposition forces, or contras, in Nicaragua.

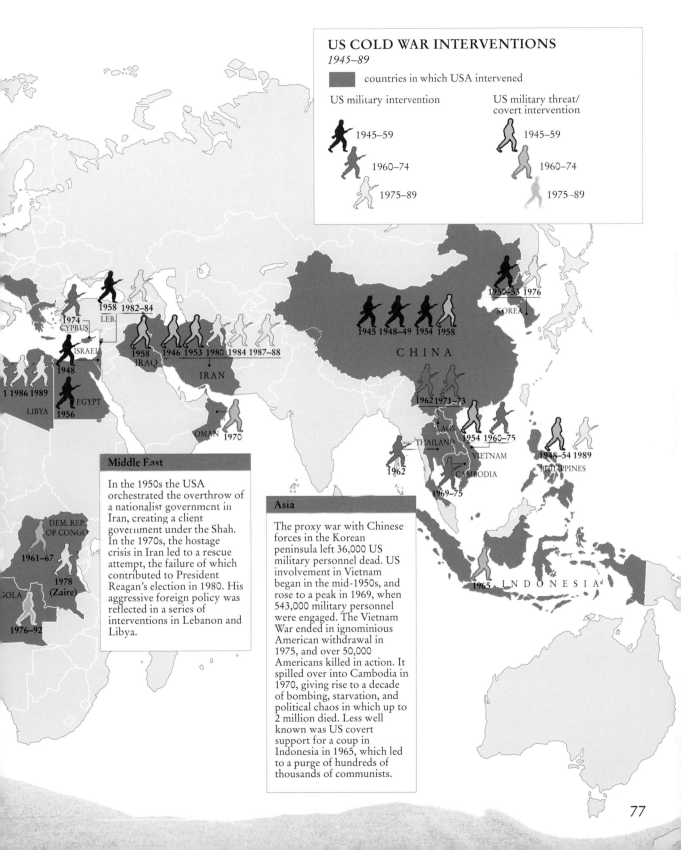

US COLD WAR INTERVENTIONS
1945–89

■ countries in which USA intervened

US military intervention

1945–59
1960–74
1975–89

US military threat/
covert intervention

1945–59
1960–74
1975–89

1950–53 1976
KOREA

1945 1948–49 1954 1958

CHINA

1958 1982–84
LEB.
1974
CYPRUS
ISRAEL
1948
1958 1946 1953 1980 1984 1987–88
IRAQ
IRAN

1 1986 1989
LIBYA
1956
EGYPT

OMAN 1970

1962 1971–73

LAOS
THAILAND 1954 1960–75
VIETNAM
1962
CAMBODIA
1969–75

1948–54 1989
PHILIPPINES

DEM. REP.
OF CONGO
1961–67
1978
(Zaire)
GOLA
1976–92

1965 INDONESIA

Middle East

In the 1950s the USA orchestrated the overthrow of a nationalist government in Iran, creating a client government under the Shah. In the 1970s, the hostage crisis in Iran led to a rescue attempt, the failure of which contributed to President Reagan's election in 1980. His aggressive foreign policy was reflected in a series of interventions in Lebanon and Libya.

Asia

The proxy war with Chinese forces in the Korean peninsula left 36,000 US military personnel dead. US involvement in Vietnam began in the mid-1950s, and rose to a peak in 1969, when 543,000 military personnel were engaged. The Vietnam War ended in ignominious American withdrawal in 1975, and over 50,000 Americans killed in action. It spilled over into Cambodia in 1970, giving rise to a decade of bombing, starvation, and political chaos in which up to 2 million died. Less well known was US covert support for a coup in Indonesia in 1965, which led to a purge of hundreds of thousands of communists.

INTERVENTIONS: 1990–2006

Since the end of the Cold War, the USA has
relied increasingly on military intervention to
implement its foreign policy.

1994–96   2004

HAITI

1990 1997 2003   LIBERIA   CÔTE
D'IVOIRE

2002

Africa

Despite multiple US
interventions in Africa, the
international community
failed to prevent genocide in
the 1990s in Rwanda, and
other humanitarian tragedies.
After terrorist bombings in
1998 in East Africa, and
missile attacks on an alleged
Al Qaeda site in Sudan in
1998, US engagement has
been driven increasingly by
the War on Terror, notably
in Somalia.

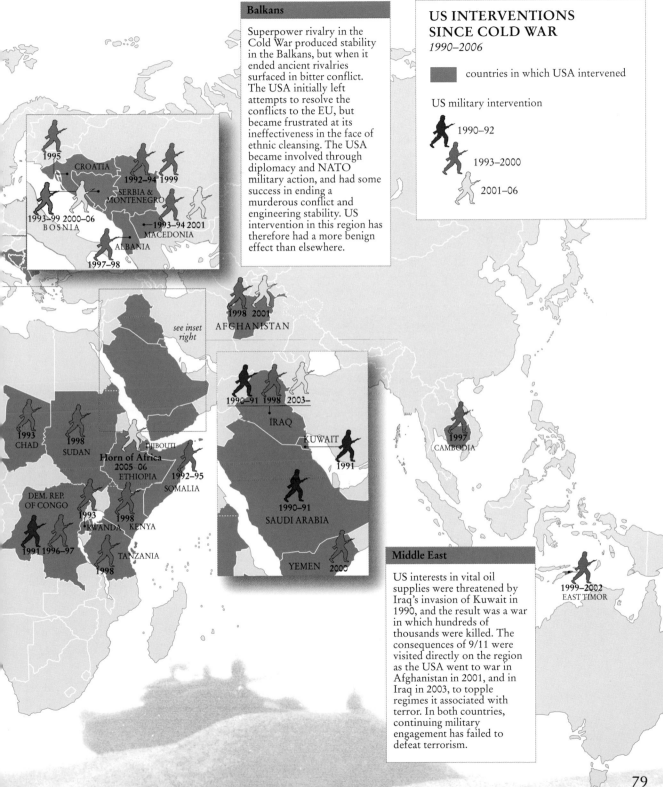

Balkans

Superpower rivalry in the Cold War produced stability in the Balkans, but when it ended ancient rivalries surfaced in bitter conflict. The USA initially left attempts to resolve the conflicts to the EU, but became frustrated at its ineffectiveness in the face of ethnic cleansing. The USA became involved through diplomacy and NATO military action, and had some success in ending a murderous conflict and engineering stability. US intervention in this region has therefore had a more benign effect than elsewhere.

US INTERVENTIONS SINCE COLD WAR
1990–2006

countries in which USA intervened

US military intervention

1990–92

1993–2000

2001–06

Balkans inset:
1995 — CROATIA
1992–94 — 1999
SERBIA & MONTENEGRO
1993–99 2000–06 — BOSNIA
1993–94 2001 — MACEDONIA
ALBANIA — 1997–98

Main map:
1998 2001 — AFGHANISTAN
see inset right
1993 — CHAD
1998 — SUDAN
DJIBOUTI
Horn of Africa 2005–06 — ETHIOPIA
1992–95 — SOMALIA
DEM. REP. OF CONGO
1993 — RWANDA
1998 — KENYA
1991 1996–97
1998 — TANZANIA
1997 — CAMBODIA

Middle East inset:
1990–91 1998 2003– — IRAQ
KUWAIT
1991
1990–91 — SAUDI ARABIA
YEMEN — 2000

1999–2002 — EAST TIMOR

Middle East

US interests in vital oil supplies were threatened by Iraq's invasion of Kuwait in 1990, and the result was a war in which hundreds of thousands were killed. The consequences of 9/11 were visited directly on the region as the USA went to war in Afghanistan in 2001, and in Iraq in 2003, to topple regimes it associated with terror. In both countries, continuing military engagement has failed to defeat terrorism.

INTERVENTIONS: MILITARY AND COVERT

Although the USA never sees itself as an aggressor, it has a long record of intervening in the internal affairs of other countries to protect its interests.

There is no simple rule to define an intervention by the USA in the affairs of another country. Its involvement has ranged from the massive engagement of the Vietnam War to activities so secret as to be imperceptible to the public eye. The biggest impact has been made by large-scale military interventions, but there has also been an almost continuous series of smaller ones, which serve to remind others of US power, and to discourage those inclined to challenge it.

Non-military interventions have been no less significant, leading to the overthrow of governments and transformations of societies. Immediately after World War II, the USA combined covert operations with a major program of aid to prevent the victory of communist parties in Greece, Italy, and Portugal. Together, these operations led to a post-war democratic, capitalist Europe.

Military force has not necessarily been more effective than covert operations in advancing US interests. The record is mixed. The Korean War (1950–53) ended in stalemate, while the Vietnam War (1960–75) was clearly a defeat. The first Gulf War (1991) ended with America securing its aims, but the aftermath of the 2003 invasion of Iraq has been disastrous for US foreign policy. Similarly, in Afghanistan, military victory has been shown to be the relatively easy part; the difficulty has been in rebuilding the society according to US ideas. Military intervention is as likely to expose the limitations of US power as to reinforce it. It is rarely sufficient to achieve policy objectives, and large-scale military interventions endanger US prestige and make defeat more significant.

Since the end of the Cold War the USA has been able to rely more on force to achieve its objectives than it did whilst under the threat of nuclear annihilation. It has reigned supreme as the world's sole superpower, and arrogance has come to characterize US foreign policy. However, there is a cycle of intervention and retrenchment in US history, and, post-Iraq, the USA is likely to pull back and rely on less belligerent means to secure its empire.

FORCES ABROAD
Number of US troops deployed
1950–2005

- Africa
- Americas
- East Asia
- Europe
- Middle East

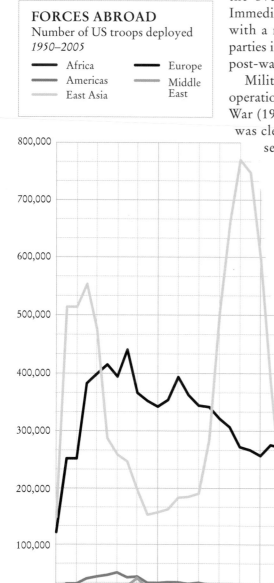

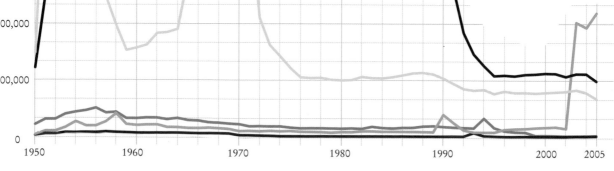

COVERT INTERVENTION: SUPPORTING BARBARIC REGIMES

Despite its claims to promote freedom and self-determination, during the Cold War, the USA intervened covertly in every decade to support barbaric regimes.

In the 1950s the CIA engineered the overthrow of the nationalist regime of Mohammad Mossadeq of Iran, ushering in an era in which the secret service, Savak, whose formation was guided by the CIA, routinely used torture to suppress all dissent to the Pahlavi regime.

After a failed coup in Indonesia in 1965, a brutal pogrom eliminated up to half a million suspected communists. The CIA provided the Indonesian regime with the names of many communist suspects.

The 1970s saw the CIA, on the orders of President Nixon, orchestrate economic sabotage, political propaganda and support for the Chilean military to contrive the overthrow of the democratically elected socialist regime of Salvador Allende. In the resulting coup of September 11, 1973, at least 5,000 people were killed, and the military junta of General Pinochet came to power.

In the 1980s, the Reagan administration provided covert support to regimes in El Salvador and Guatemala that ruled with unspeakable brutality, using death squads, including military officers trained at the notorious US-based School of the Americas, in massacres in which 70,000 people were killed.

It is impossible to know exactly the consequences of these covert operations, conducted mostly by the CIA, but the toll in death and misery rivals that associated with direct US military action in the post-war era.

MILITARY INTERVENTION: IRAQ

Many argue that George W. Bush came into office determined to complete the business unfinished by his father, who left Saddam Hussein in power in 1991, and that 9/11 was a convenient rationale for a predetermined course of action, rather than a reaction to the threat posed by terrorism. The revelation that the threat posed by Saddam holding weapons of mass destruction was specious adds credence to this assertion.

There are two further reasons to believe that the invasion of Iraq was pre-meditated. First, in contrast to the first Gulf War, when George Bush Sr. took great care to build a multilateral coalition through the United Nations, and developed a model for post-Cold-War policing that was genuinely non-imperial, prior to the second war, the United Nations was manipulated and treated with contempt, and the USA acted much more unilaterally and imperially.

The second reason is that, while both interventions had a common principal motive – securing supplies of oil – it has become apparent that overthrowing Saddam was only the first step in a plan to transform the Middle East. The goals of the first war were more circumscribed and the more successful for it. In both, military victory was achieved, but in the second the military was asked to take on a nation-building role for which they were ill-equipped.

The lessons are that multilateralism works better than unilateralism, especially in winning the peace, and grandiose attempts to impose democracy from the outside are a contradiction in terms that bring only opprobrium on the aggressor.

THE PACIFIC RIM

With many of the world's leading powers emerging in the region, the Pacific Rim is likely to become the main focus of US foreign policy.

The USA sees itself as preventing a potentially unstable Asia from descending into conflict by striking a balance between the various great nations of the region. The US-led reconstruction of Japan after World War II was such a success that by the 1990s many felt that US protection of Japan had spawned its own replacement as a super-state. These fears have receded as the Japanese economic juggernaut has slowed down.

China has now replaced Japan as the potential challenger to the American empire, both militarily and economically. It is a sign of the changing balance of power in Asia that China's restraining influence over the regime in North Korea is becoming increasingly important.

India is coming up fast in the great power stakes. After years of tense relations, the USA has begun to cultivate the country, hoping to use a friendly India as a counterweight to Chinese hegemony in Asia. The flexibility of the American approach to the sub-continent is part of a strategy to preserve the USA's power in the face of increased competition from the East.

National Security Strategy

National Security Strategy under George W. Bush has taken on an expansionist and aggressive posture. Publicly formulated in the policy statement of 2002, it is clearly intended to ensure that the USA retains its imperial status.

There are two major elements:

- The USA will not allow any nation to challenge its military pre-eminence, and pre-emptive force can and should be used to head off imminent threats.

- World security will only exist when all countries share the administration's view of terror. Removal of regimes with a different perspective therefore becomes imperative.

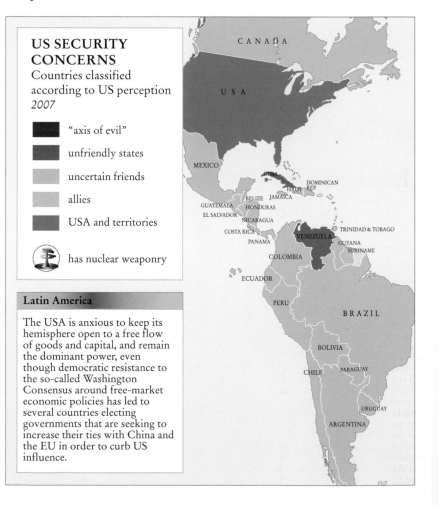

US SECURITY CONCERNS
Countries classified according to US perception
2007

- "axis of evil"
- unfriendly states
- uncertain friends
- allies
- USA and territories
- has nuclear weaponry

Latin America

The USA is anxious to keep its hemisphere open to a free flow of goods and capital, and remain the dominant power, even though democratic resistance to the so-called Washington Consensus around free-market economic policies has led to several countries electing governments that are seeking to increase their ties with China and the EU in order to curb US influence.

On the eastern side of the Pacific Rim, Latin America has long been near the bottom of the USA's list of foreign-policy priorities, mainly because, being more in control of this region than of any other, it feels less threatened by it. Increasing cooperation between South American countries and China and Japan does, however, pose a potential threat to the USA.

India and Pakistan

As part of a strategy for balance and stability in Asia, the USA is hoping to defuse tension between these two rivals. The USA has adopted a flexible approach, concluding an unprecedented agreement with India on the sharing of nuclear technology, while ensuring the continued co-operation of Pakistan in the fight against terrorism.

North and South Korea

The tension between North and South Korea, which has persisted since the armistice of 1953, is in danger of being destabilized by North Korea's announcement in 2006 that it had tested nuclear weapons. The USA offered economic concessions if North Korea relinquished its program. China, which has the greatest influence over the regime of North Korea, has also urged restraint.

Japan

The USA and Japan have a common security interest in curbing the rise of China. Japan is seen by many in the USA as a force for stability in Asia; in return the USA will maintain its security umbrella over Japan, despite the desire of some Japanese to become less dependent on the USA.

China

While remaining firm on issues such as the status of Taiwan, the USA is drawing China into the world trading system, and developing a relationship of mutual interdependence that it is hoped will reduce the risk of conflict. US policy is a mixture of firmness and accommodation, but a more flexible approach would be the best way to preserve US power, and that view is gaining the upper hand. Too much aggression would encourage China to develop new anti-American alliances around the world, a policy some in the USA suspect it is already pursuing.

Compacts of Free Association

After World War II the USA was tasked with steering the Northern Marianas, Federated States of Micronesia (FSM), Republic of the Marshall Islands (RMI), and Palau towards independence. Keeping the islands economically dependent suited the USA, however, because it allowed it to establish a military presence in the western Pacific, and prevented other nations from doing so. In the 1980s the USA developed Compacts of Free Association with the FSM and RMI, providing them with millions of dollars, and internal self-government, in exchange for US military rights.

In 1981, as part of the process towards self-government, Palau, mindful of the effects of nuclear tests in the neighbouring Marshall Islands, adopted a constitution with a nuclear-free clause. The USA imposed successive referenda on the people of Palau to overthrow the clause and agree the Compact. In 1985, the first President, Haruo Remeliik, an advocate of the nuclear-free clause, was assassinated. The second, Lazarus Salii, apparently committed suicide in 1988, after being placed under investigation for accepting political payoffs while Minister responsible for Compact negotiations. The islanders voted more than 10 times before finally agreeing to a Compact in 1994, the economic terms of which are due for renewal in 2009. The options on military use will last until 2044, and the security provisions will continue indefinitely unless mutually terminated.

EUROPE, MIDDLE EAST AND AFRICA

Although the threat to US security from the ex-Soviet Union has disappeared, new threats have emerged from the Middle East.

During the Cold War the principal goal of US security policy was to neutralize the threat to Europe from the Soviet Union. This was achieved when the Soviet Union collapsed in 1991, and in the following decade the USA's main challenge was to ensure the emergence of a peaceful Russia and other former communist states from the rubble of the USSR. American support for market capitalism in post-communist Russia was more effective in bringing about mafia capitalism than effective democracy, but the denuclearization of several ex-Soviet states was the unsung triumph of the Clinton administration.

The European Union has maintained a fundamentally close relationship with the USA, even without the perceived threat of invasion by the communist East. And although European views on many major world issues differ from those of the USA, the EU has not cohered sufficiently to challenge American pre-eminence in global affairs.

The difference between the American and European perspective is especially apparent in the Middle East, which has replaced Europe as the primary focus of US foreign policy in recent years. The region contains both America's greatest friend – Israel – and potentially its greatest foe – Iran – and the growth of anti-American radicalism threatens US strategic interests.

Not all areas of the world pose a security threat to the USA, however. Humanitarian crises arising from war, ethnic conflict, terrorism, famine and HIV/AIDS have dominated Africa in recent years, and America's reaction, along with that of other western powers, has not been successful in combating them. Failure to prevent impoverishment, especially in Muslim Africa, may result in radicalism that would feed into existing threats to US national security.

Nuclear threat

The USA's nuclear arsenal remains vital to its security even though it is no longer threatened by full-scale attack from another nation state. The greatest threat now comes from covert operations against Americans at home or abroad, carried out by terrorist groups supported by what the USA considers "rogue states". The possession of a nuclear capability by these states is therefore of immense concern to the USA.

The USA clearly applies double standards. While it is unconcerned by the fact that its allies have a nuclear capacity, it sees the potential for nuclear capacity in non-allies as a pretext for intervention or even invasion. These non-allies cannot accept that they should not themselves hold nuclear weapons, and feel increasingly threatened by the USA. US attempts to maintain nuclear supremacy are leading others to seek nuclear protection from US power.

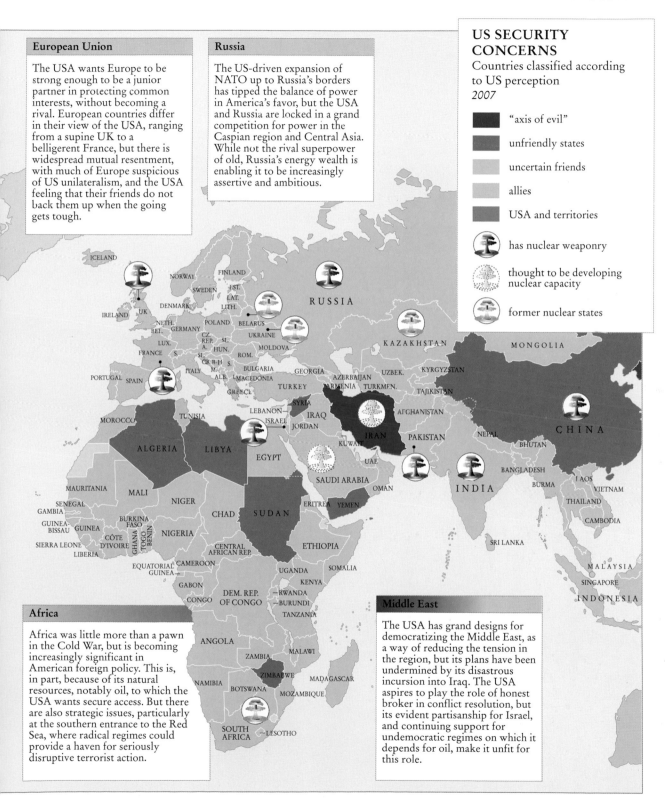

European Union

The USA wants Europe to be strong enough to be a junior partner in protecting common interests, without becoming a rival. European countries differ in their view of the USA, ranging from a supine UK to a belligerent France, but there is widespread mutual resentment, with much of Europe suspicious of US unilateralism, and the USA feeling that their friends do not back them up when the going gets tough.

Russia

The US-driven expansion of NATO up to Russia's borders has tipped the balance of power in America's favor, but the USA and Russia are locked in a grand competition for power in the Caspian region and Central Asia. While not the rival superpower of old, Russia's energy wealth is enabling it to be increasingly assertive and ambitious.

US SECURITY CONCERNS

Countries classified according to US perception
2007

- "axis of evil"
- unfriendly states
- uncertain friends
- allies
- USA and territories

- has nuclear weaponry
- thought to be developing nuclear capacity
- former nuclear states

Africa

Africa was little more than a pawn in the Cold War, but is becoming increasingly significant in American foreign policy. This is, in part, because of its natural resources, notably oil, to which the USA wants secure access. But there are also strategic issues, particularly at the southern entrance to the Red Sea, where radical regimes could provide a haven for seriously disruptive terrorist action.

Middle East

The USA has grand designs for democratizing the Middle East, as a way of reducing the tension in the region, but its plans have been undermined by its disastrous incursion into Iraq. The USA aspires to play the role of honest broker in conflict resolution, but its evident partisanship for Israel, and continuing support for undemocratic regimes on which it depends for oil, make it unfit for this role.

Chapter Seven
SOFT POWER

The USA exercises power through a range of instruments. At one end of the spectrum is military power, but this can be a sign of policy failure as force is not effective in the long term. Other instruments include aid, which is used not just for humanitarian relief, but to influence government policy in recipient countries.

Leadership of international financial institutions is a means of extending US influence over the world economy, and participation in other non-economic international agencies, such as the United Nations, serve the same purpose of extending US power. America has an ambivalent relationship to such organizations, not wishing to have its actions circumscribed by external control. Where international organizations threaten its sovereignty, the USA is powerful enough to be able simply to opt out, as it has done with the International Criminal Court, whose jurisdiction over US nationals it does not recognize. Power is also exercised through informal networks linking the upper levels of business and government. These contacts form an elite that works to create international consensus on major issues before they are translated into government policy.

Soft power is most closely associated with winning hearts and minds – encouraging others to share US values and to see its policies as legitimate. American culture – ranging from the democratic vigor of its political institutions, through to the glamour of Hollywood, and the attractions of its consumer culture – has a strong magnetic attraction across the world. But the goodwill and admiration that this culture might inspire is dissipated by the policies of the US government. The USA is losing legitimacy among those who see it as a bullying, interfering country, rather than one to be emulated. Competing world views, such as European social democracy, Chinese non-interference, or Islamism are developing wider appeal.

In the 1990s the USA appeared to embody the aspirations of much of the world, but this legacy has been squandered by the unilateral policies of the 21st century and, above all, by the debacle in Iraq.

> " HE THAT GIVES GOOD ADMONITION AND BAD EXAMPLE, BUILDS WITH ONE HAND AND PULLS DOWN WITH THE OTHER. "
>
> FRANCIS BACON
> ENGLISH PHILOSOPHER
> (1561–1626)

AID AND INFLUENCE

US aid is an arm of foreign policy, and its distribution is closely tied to US economic and security priorities.

The driving force behind US aid is the security and economic policy of America, rather than humanitarian need. Military and security assistance for countries involved in the War on Terror makes up one-third of all US foreign aid – roughly matching that at the height of the Cold War in the 1980s. When all forms of aid are taken into account, aid to the Middle East dwarfs that given to any other region, with Israel receiving the lion's share.

The USA is by far the largest donor of official development assistance, but gives less relative to the size of its economy than almost any other OECD country. The amount requested by the administration of George W. Bush for foreign aid was, typically, only 5 percent of that spent on defense, and was exceeded by donations from American individuals, corporations, foundations, and religious groups.

The USA increased its aid in 2005, reflecting mounting concern among OECD countries about global poverty, but a third of the increase went to Afghanistan and Iraq, demonstrating how aid follows the priorities of US foreign policy and the humanitarian crises it creates.

The financial value of the aid given is not necessarily a guide to its effectiveness in tackling poverty. The form of aid given is determined largely by US domestic political and economic conditions, rather than by identified needs in recipient countries. Around 70 percent is actually spent on US goods and services, with aid recipients obliged to purchase these at uncompetitive prices. The effect is evident in the failure to decrease poverty, something often blamed, incorrectly, on mismanagement by receiving countries.

Aid in the form of loans can tie countries into a dependency that gives the USA leverage over their domestic and foreign policies. This is often the determinant of aid policy, rather than the altruistic motives that are its ostensible rationale.

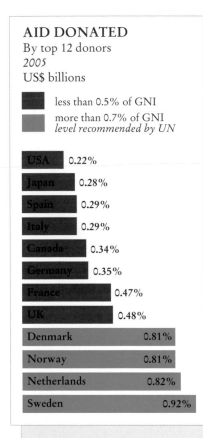

AID DONATED
By top 12 donors
2005
US$ billions

■ less than 0.5% of GNI
■ more than 0.7% of GNI
level recommended by UN

USA	0.22%
Japan	0.28%
Spain	0.29%
Italy	0.29%
Canada	0.34%
Germany	0.35%
France	0.47%
UK	0.48%
Denmark	0.81%
Norway	0.81%
Netherlands	0.82%
Sweden	0.92%

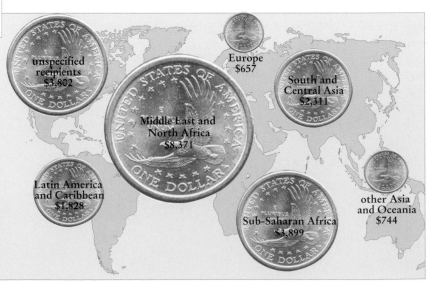

unspecified recipients $3,802

Europe $657

South and Central Asia $2,311

Middle East and North Africa $8,371

Latin America and Caribbean $1,828

Sub-Saharan Africa $3,899

other Asia and Oceania $744

US OVERSEAS DEVELOPMENT AID
by region and largest recipient countries
2003–05 average
US$ millions

FOREIGN MILITARY FINANCING

Most US arms exports are financed by an "aid" package. Foreign Military Finance is the main vehicle for this, providing grants for the acquisition of US defense equipment, services, and training. These grants are intended to improve US national security by increasing the defense capabilities of friendly governments and combating transnational threats, including terrorism and trafficking.

As in previous years, in 2005 Israel received by far the largest amount of bilateral foreign military finance, closely followed by Egypt.

The promise of bilateral military aid is a powerful lever that the USA uses to influence the wider policies of the recipient countries, trading military supplies for support from recipients in diverse areas, including environmental policy.

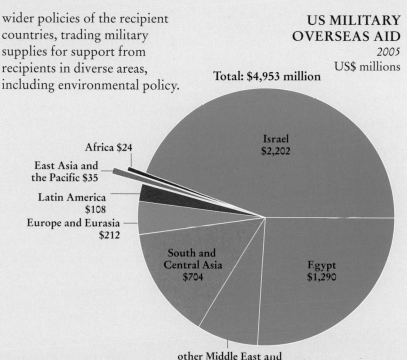

US MILITARY OVERSEAS AID
2005
US$ millions

Total: $4,953 million

Israel $2,202
Africa $24
East Asia and the Pacific $35
Latin America $108
Europe and Eurasia $212
South and Central Asia $704
Egypt $1,290
other Middle East and North Africa $378

FOOD AID

The USA gave over $1bn to the UN World Food Programme (WFP) in 2004, making it the largest donor. It also distributes its own international food aid via programs that provide emergency assistance, and claim to develop trade, promote security, and economic development.

In the 1990s, much aid went to Russia, with the aim of creating a stable and democratic trading partner. The focus is now on emergency relief. Valuable as this can be in relieving hunger, it has to be seen in the context of US domestic agricultural policy. The USA heavily subsidizes its own industrial-scale farms, creating surplus agricultural products that its domestic producers eagerly off-load on to food aid schemes. This introduces a level of uncertainty into the supply of aid that can distort global trade patterns and depress local prices.

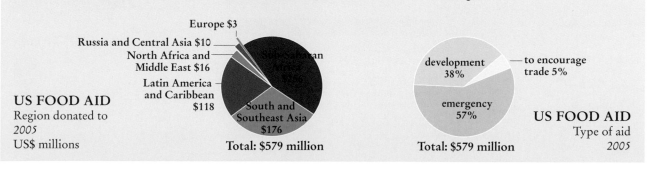

Europe $3
Russia and Central Asia $10
North Africa and Middle East $16
Latin America and Caribbean $118
Sub-Saharan Africa $256
South and Southeast Asia $176

US FOOD AID
Region donated to
2005
US$ millions

Total: $579 million

development 38%
to encourage trade 5%
emergency 57%

Total: $579 million

US FOOD AID
Type of aid
2005

RELATIONS WITH THE UN

The relationship between the USA and the UN is one of mutual suspicion and, in recent times, of hostility.

The USA played a prominent part in founding the UN, and remains its chief financial contributor, but will not allow it to influence US foreign policy. However, the UN does not bend as easily to American pressure as do some of the other international organizations through which the USA extends its influence. Indeed, the UN's multilateral and consensual management of the international system represents the main alternative to the American Empire as a system of global governance.

Even though the vehement anti-UN sentiment expressed by America's Neo-Conservatives is not reflected in US public opinion, in the post-Iraq unilateralist phase of US foreign policy, the UN, and what it stands for, is anathema. In practice, however, the relationship is more ambivalent: the UN gives the USA a cloak of international legitimacy, and the USA provides force and effectiveness which the UN would otherwise lack.

A stable relationship between the USA and the UN is unlikely. The USA will not give up control of its policies, and the member states of the UN will not refrain from criticizing US actions. When there is a meeting of interests, there will be co-operation; when there is not, the USA will go it alone or will use other agencies, such as NATO, and the UN will be unable to stop it.

The USA provides 17% of the budget for UN peacekeeping, but only 0.4% of the personnel. It is unwilling to recognize any supranational authority in matters of armed conflict. If the USA commits a large number of troops, it invariably retains control, directly or through NATO. Moreover, US troops are unfitted to peacekeeping. Their mentality and training better suits them to fighting, and their identification with US foreign policy makes their presence contentious in a field where consensus building is of the essence.

PEACEKEEPING AND PEACEMAKING
Selected operations
1991–2006

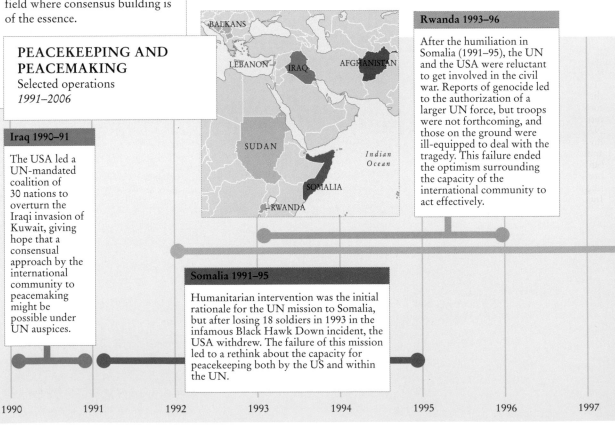

Iraq 1990–91

The USA led a UN-mandated coalition of 30 nations to overturn the Iraqi invasion of Kuwait, giving hope that a consensual approach by the international community to peacemaking might be possible under UN auspices.

Rwanda 1993–96

After the humiliation in Somalia (1991–95), the UN and the USA were reluctant to get involved in the civil war. Reports of genocide led to the authorization of a larger UN force, but troops were not forthcoming, and those on the ground were ill-equipped to deal with the tragedy. This failure ended the optimism surrounding the capacity of the international community to act effectively.

Somalia 1991–95

Humanitarian intervention was the initial rationale for the UN mission to Somalia, but after losing 18 soldiers in 1993 in the infamous Black Hawk Down incident, the USA withdrew. The failure of this mission led to a rethink about the capacity for peacekeeping both by the US and within the UN.

| 1990 | 1991 | 1992 | 1993 | 1994 | 1995 | 1996 | 1997 |

UN FINANCES

Despite its difficult relationship to the UN, the USA remains by far the biggest financial contributor. Each member state is required to pay a levy under the UN Charter. In 2001 the General Assembly, after US pressure, capped the maximum contribution at 22 percent of the total budget. This reduced the required US contribution, which had previously been set at about 25 percent of the budget. Even though its assessed contribution has declined, the USA remains heavily in arrears with its payments. The size of the US contribution gives it leverage over UN actions and the practice of withholding of funds increases this.

UN FUNDING

Largest contributors' annual assessment of contribution 2006
US$ millions

USA	$423
Japan	$332
Germany	$148
UK	$105
France	$103
Italy	$83
Canada	$48
Spain	$43
China	$35
Mexico	$32
South Korea	$31

CUMULATIVE ARREARS

Amount owed to UN by USA and other countries
year end 1996–2005
US$ millions

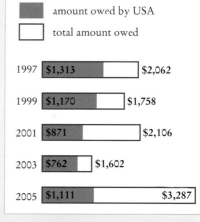

▨ amount owed by USA
☐ total amount owed

	amount owed by USA	total amount owed
1997	$1,313	$2,062
1999	$1,170	$1,758
2001	$871	$2,106
2003	$762	$1,602
2005	$1,111	$3,287

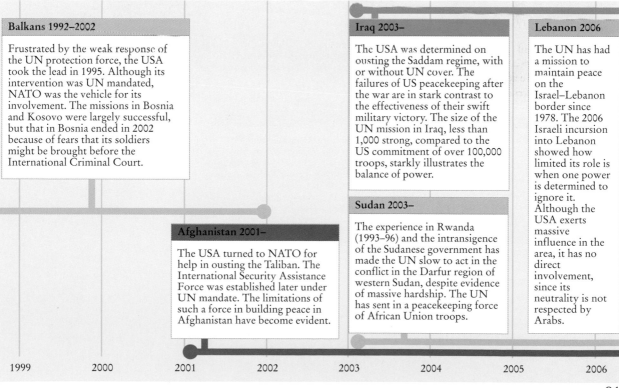

Balkans 1992–2002

Frustrated by the weak response of the UN protection force, the USA took the lead in 1995. Although its intervention was UN mandated, NATO was the vehicle for its involvement. The missions in Bosnia and Kosovo were largely successful, but that in Bosnia ended in 2002 because of fears that its soldiers might be brought before the International Criminal Court.

Afghanistan 2001–

The USA turned to NATO for help in ousting the Taliban. The International Security Assistance Force was established later under UN mandate. The limitations of such a force in building peace in Afghanistan have become evident.

Iraq 2003–

The USA was determined on ousting the Saddam regime, with or without UN cover. The failures of US peacekeeping after the war are in stark contrast to the effectiveness of their swift military victory. The size of the UN mission in Iraq, less than 1,000 strong, compared to the US commitment of over 100,000 troops, starkly illustrates the balance of power.

Sudan 2003–

The experience in Rwanda (1993–96) and the intransigence of the Sudanese government has made the UN slow to act in the conflict in the Darfur region of western Sudan, despite evidence of massive hardship. The UN has sent in a peacekeeping force of African Union troops.

Lebanon 2006

The UN has had a mission to maintain peace on the Israel–Lebanon border since 1978. The 2006 Israeli incursion into Lebanon showed how limited its role is when one power is determined to ignore it. Although the USA exerts massive influence in the area, it has no direct involvement, since its neutrality is not respected by Arabs.

1999	2000	2001	2002	2003	2004	2005	2006

The IMF and World Bank extend the influence of America's free-market philosophy around the world.

The USA exercises control over the world economic system by working with and through others. Despite its unilateral tendencies, it could never guarantee the global order on its own. International Financial Institutions (IFIs) have been vital to the USA as a means of managing crises in, and co-ordination of, the world economy, and of ensuring continued access to markets for wealthy countries. These organizations, while not ostensibly under US control, are a vital arm of US imperial power, extending US influence beyond the confines of inter-state relations.

The World Bank helps to further US interests in the field of development aid. Although a multilateral organization, it is always headed by a nominee of the US administration, and has consistently pursued policies compatible with, indeed dictated by, the US agenda for developing countries.

The International Monetary Fund (IMF)has been even more influential in pushing the Washington Neo-Liberal Agenda in recent years. The USA is the leading voice in a group of advanced capitalist

World Bank

The World Bank is a major source of financial assistance to developing countries, with a mission to reduce global poverty and commitments of over $23 billion in 2006. World Bank loans come with an insistence on economic liberalization and a reduced role for the state. They undermine national sovereignty, create a burden of debt, and are often unsuitable for less developed societies experiencing conflicts or dictatorship.

Because the Bank is seen to promote US priorities and interests, many of the more advanced developing countries, such as Brazil, China, Indonesia, and Mexico, are going elsewhere for their loans without their growth rates appearing to suffer. As a result of this, and of the recent initiatives on debt relief, World Bank income from borrowers' fees has halved since 2000.

Some Western countries have advocated that the Bank stop requiring economic reforms in countries that do not want them and concentrate instead on increasing debt relief. Reforms of this kind are necessary if the Bank is not to become an irrelevance in the process of world economic development.

USA

The USA contributes 17% of IMF and World Bank funds – more than twice that of any other contributor – and effectively holds the power of veto over major decisions. The USA nominates the Director of the World Bank. The director appointed in 2005, Paul Wolfowitz, is a former US Deputy Secretary of Defense. His appointments of Bank staff raised fears he would politicize lending decisions, for example by supporting US objectives in the Middle East rather than pressing humanitarian need in Africa.

Latin America

In 2001 Argentina defaulted on debt repayments. The IMF rescue package dictated privatization, selling of assets and cuts in government spending. As Argentina sank into economic depression, its government refused to pay more than a proportion of its debts. The Fund backed down and Argentina, along with Brazil, has subsequently paid off all its debt. The trend towards left-wing governments in Latin America has been ascribed to the lessons learned from the Argentine crisis.

IMF AND WORLD BANK INTERVENTIONS
since 1991

nations that exert significant control over the economic policies of developing countries through loans administered by the IMF. The conditions attached to these loans put the interests of international capital and the stability of markets ahead of the needs of the poor of the receiving countries.

Effective as they have been in serving the American empire, the IFIs are in crisis. Borrowing countries are rebelling against the onerous conditions on which aid is granted. If they refuse to become indebted to the IMF or World Bank, they escape the control of these institutions and regain control of their destiny. Until now the IFIs have been more concerned with the interests of the powerful non-borrowing members than with those of their clients. This will have to change.

IMF

The original purpose of the IMF was to maintain international economic stability by lending to countries with balance of payments difficulties, but the conditions attached to IMF loans invariably include privatization. This offers international capital the chance to buy assets cheaply, but exposes borrowing countries to capital flight, and leads to exorbitant interest rates that decimate the domestic economy. Borrowers are also required to cut the size of the state sector and eliminate subsidies, measures that lower the standard of living of the poor. Although IMF prescriptions have drawn poor countries into the global market, they have increased inequality, poverty and indebtedness.

Increasingly, however, poor countries are turning to private markets or to countries such as China, leading to a halving in repayments to the IMF between 2005 and 2006, with further falls predicted.

Russia and Central Asia

After communism collapsed, the IMF, with strong US backing, dictated privatization to reconstruct the Russian economy. Selling off of state assets led to soaring corruption, national output was almost halved and in 1998 Russia defaulted on its debt in a financial collapse widely attributed to IMF policies. Subsequent improvements in Russia's economy have been based on its energy resources rather than the IMF. IFI assistance is now targeted on the ex-Soviet countries in Central Asia, where World Bank lending reached $4 billion in 2006, focused on reducing corruption.

Sub-Saharan Africa

Structural adjustment programs have failed to promote growth, and charging patients for healthcare has contributed to Africa's inability to deal with the HIV/AIDS pandemic. Corruption has been blamed for the failure of aid schemes, diverting attention from the fact that debt servicing has taken priority over the needs of African people. The World Bank has begun to implement debt relief, but many countries are looking elsewhere, notably to China, for assistance.

South-East and East Asia

In 1997 Asian economies were forced to turn to the IMF, which lent $36 billion. The loan conditions served the interests of western creditors, enforcing privatization and liberalization that made East Asian economies vulnerable to speculative capital, and imposing cuts that harmed their economic and social fabric. Subsequently, Asian countries have paid off their debts, refrained from new borrowing and regained financial sovereignty.

93

INFORMAL NETWORKS

Informal networks help to extend US power by creating a consensus among the world's economic and political elites in support of America's world view.

The foreign policy of the USA, and therefore its impact on the world, is influenced by a complex overlapping network of informal agencies.

Think tanks are a major source of ideas for the Washington policy-making process. There are dozens of independent institutes, and many more located in universities. Their approach reflects the entire US political spectrum, and many of the most influential ideas arise from organizations closely associated with the party in opposition. They provide the intellectual capital needed by a prospective administration, and are, in effect, an "administration in waiting".

Lobby groups exist to pressure government officials and elected politicians on specific policies. Most are oriented to domestic policies, but some are also effective in influencing foreign policy. Lobby groups not only create policy, but provide the public rationale for those policies. The clearest example is the influence of the pro-Israeli lobby on America's Middle East policy.

American Israel Public Affairs Committee

AIPAC works to steer US foreign policy in a pro-Israeli direction – its success is evident from the support US administrations have given to Israel. Its power is enhanced by support from Christian Evangelicals, who see Israel as fulfilling biblical prophecy, and support its expansionist agenda.

Brookings Institution

This center-left think tank aims to develop sound public policies and promote public understanding of issues of national importance. Its work is widely cited.

The Center for Strategic and International Studies

A strategic planning partner for the government, it conducts research and analysis and develops policy initiatives that look into the future and anticipate change.

Council on Foreign Relations

This membership organization aims to increase US understanding of the world by contributing ideas to foreign policy through research, debates, and the journal *Foreign Affairs*. It is at the more liberal end of establishment politics.

The Defense Policy Board Advisory Committee

This provides the Secretary of Defense with advice on issues central to strategic planning. Its influential former chairman, Richard Perle, was one of the architects of the policies of George W. Bush.

Heritage Foundation

Its stated mission, like that of fellow right-of-centre think tank, the American Enterprise Institute, is to formulate and promote conservative public policies, based on a strong national defense. It was the architect of the 1980s Reagan Doctrine, and has been supportive of the policies of George W. Bush.

Project for the New American Century

The goal of this educational organization, established during the Clinton years, is to promote the USA's world leadership, which critics interpret as a blueprint for global domination. Some 20 of its members took up positions within the administration of George W. Bush, including the Vice President and the Secretary of Defense. As a strong advocate of the invasion of Iraq, its reputation has been somewhat tarnished.

THINK TANKS AND LOBBIES

Rand Corporation

Originally a scientific advisory service for the US armed forces, it also now provides advice to other governments and to commercial organizations, and has 1,600 employees in the USA and Europe. It develops systems analysis, and about half of its work is on issues of national security. Much of this is classified, which gives rise to concern about the nature of the advice it gives.

Other groups provide a means by which informal understandings and bonds are cemented among the powerful, both inside the USA and internationally. They create policy, through meetings and research projects, but their most important role is to create a common world view among their members. They provide an opportunity for business, in particular, to influence policy-makers by developing close personal relationships that are built up outside government but are often vital when members enter government. These organizations are transnational, although they remain largely Anglo-American and Eurocentric, and are vital to the creation of an international ruling class that shares personal contacts, loyalties, and intellectual perceptions vital to effective government in a globalized world.

By their nature, these associations are often secretive, giving rise to conspiracy theories and charges that they amount to a secret world government that dictates to elected representatives. The truth is more prosaic, but none the less vital for that.

INFORMAL NETWORKS

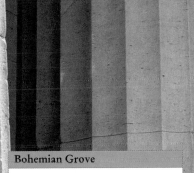

G8

The group started meeting in the 1970s as a world economic summit, but now provides an opportunity for heads of government to discuss a wide range of issues without the formality normally associated with top-level inter-government relations. Membership is centered on North America, Europe (including Russia), and Japan, and does not include some of the main economic players.

Kissinger Associates

Founded by Henry Kissinger in 1982, the firm assists a select group of multinational companies to identify strategic partners and investment opportunities, using the foreign-policy experience of its associates to facilitate relations with overseas governments. The company does not disclose the names of its corporate clients but they are thought to include Coca-Cola and American Express.

Trilateral Commission

Formed to foster closer co-operation between Japan, Europe, and North America, its membership has broadened to include China. It includes about 350 leaders in media, academia, public service, labor unions, and other non-governmental organizations, but excludes those currently holding government positions. It is an influential grooming ground for emerging political leaders.

Bohemian Grove

This is the site of an annual "summer camp" to which a secret list of leading figures from within the USA and beyond are invited. Members have included every US president since Kennedy, cabinet officials, and heads of large corporations, including banks, military contractors, oil companies, and the media. It is an elaborate bonding ritual that has attracted much suspicion.

World Economic Forum

This independent international organization shapes global, regional and industrial agendas. It operates under the supervision of the Swiss government but also has an American national association. It holds an annual meeting of top business and political leaders and selected intellectuals and journalists, usually in Davos, Switzerland.

Bilderberg Group

This informal network creates connections between Europe and North America. It meets at an invitation-only annual conference of about 100 leading figures in business, politics, the media, and academia. The agenda is public, but the discussions are off the record, inviting speculation as to what is discussed, agreed, and decided when people of such power congregate.

Carlyle Group

The largest investment firm in Washington DC, managing billions of dollars of equity capital, it specializes in politically sensitive areas, such as aerospace, and has interests in several military contractors, and in contracts with Saudi Arabia. Both George W. Bush and his father have been associates.

Chapter Eight

IDEAS

Ideas matter in the maintenance of the American empire, because the USA's rationale for its policies is that it acts both to further its own interests and to promote freedom across the world. The wars in Afghanistan and Iraq, and the War on Terror, have been justified as battles of ideas, and American power has been projected as an instrument of divine will and as a triumph over evil. This imperial mentality tramples on the sensibilities of those without the law, and leaves the USA open to charges of hypocrisy when its actions appear to have baser motivations than the lofty ideals it employs to defend them.

Although the USA works hard to convey a positive image through its public diplomacy, its status as an exemplar of modernity is being eroded. The USA has contributed to its fall from grace by exporting an ideology of nationalism, human rights, and democracy that provides the basis for a critique of its own world role. National self-determination, of which Islamism is a variant, has strong legitimacy, so when America's confrontation with other nations is graphically disseminated through global media it erodes American legitimacy.

The gap between America's self conception and how others see it has widened. Where America sees defense, others see aggression; where it sees openness and tolerance, others see insularity, arrogance, and piety; where it sees principle, others see naked self-interest; and, where once there was widespread admiration of American values and standards of living, now there is resentment and anger at its attempt to coral all others in its own image. With such a gap it is not surprising that other cultures are fighting back and challenging the right to leadership previously enjoyed by the USA.

> " WORLD POLITICS IS ENTERING A NEW PHASE, IN WHICH THE GREAT DIVISIONS AMONG HUMANKIND AND THE DOMINATING SOURCE OF INTERNATIONAL CONFLICT WILL BE CULTURAL.
>
> SAMUEL P. HUNTINGTON, AMERICAN POLITICAL SCIENTIST 1993

How America Sees the World

Most Americans are not isolationist. They support the role their government plays in the world.

The way in which a nation exercises its power is influenced, in part, by how it sees itself. America, as a society founded on rebellion against the corruption of the old world, views itself as representing the ability to create a more perfect society. Most Americans see their values and institutions as an example to others, and their way of life as something to which others should universally aspire. The danger arises when this self-admiration extends to a desire to impose the American social model on to other cultures.

Americans are so convinced of the superiority of their own system they have difficulty appreciating the virtues of others. Convinced of the nobility of their motives and generosity of spirit, they cannot comprehend how their actions can be perceived as aggressive or exploitative, or indeed imperial. At its worst, Americans see alternative cultures as embodiments of evil, and combating them as a duty to

Terrorism, not surprisingly, is seen as the most serious threat to the USA. Americans are also concerned about Islamic fundamentalism, although most distinguish between the fanaticism of a few, and the attitude of mainstream Muslims, with whom they believe there is common ground. Global warming is seen as a threat, but most Americans feel that international co-operation is needed to combat it. Americans tend to have a positive attitude to globalization, indicating a willingness to integrate with the world, and 75% of Americans accept that the USA should comply with rulings by the World Trade Organization, even when these go against the USA.

PERCEIVED SECURITY THREATS

Percentage of Americans who see these issues as a critical threat to US interest in the next 10 years
2006

international terrorism	74%
nuclear proliferation	69%
energy supply	59%
immigration	51%
epidemics	49%
global warming	46%
Islamic fundamentalism	43%
instability in Korea	38%
China	36%
economic competition	32%

protecting American jobs	76%
preventing nuclear proliferation	74%
combating terrorism	72%
securing energy supplies	72%
promoting economic growth	62%
controlling immigration	58%
maintaining US military power	55%
improving the global environment	54%
combating world hunger	48%
strengthening the United Nations	40%
promoting human rights abroad	28%
spreading democracy	17%

US FOREIGN POLICY GOALS

Percentage of Americans who think these goals should be a priority
2006

Despite welcoming globalization, Americans are concerned about its effect on their jobs. Other priorities match perceived threats to the USA, with national security and the environment prominent. Commitment to internationalism is apparent in a supportive attitude to UN humanitarian interventions. There is support for the use of US troops abroad for humanitarian operations, and to stop the spread of nuclear weapons, but not for direct intervention in conflicts between other nation states.

civilize a world corrupted by false gods. As a result, the USA often lacks the respect and restraint necessary when dealing with sovereign states, and instead is a mirror image of a radical, proselytizing Islam.

The events of 9/11 reinforced these tendencies, and many non-Americans now see the USA as having embarked on nothing less than a religiously inspired crusade to impose American values on the world. The result is a clash of civilizations, revolving around a gap in perceptions, beliefs, and ideas that is the principal dynamic in international affairs today.

Most Americans want to pursue their foreign policy goals chiefly through co-operative and multilateral means. Despite recognizing that the USA is the sole superpower, Americans reject a world order based on a single power. They prefer an international system, in which power is shared among nations and the UN has a significant role. Even so, they continue to support a strong American military presence around the world and are willing to take unilateral action where they believe US interests are at stake.

CHINA

Although a small minority of Americans view China as an outright enemy, and strong majorities disapprove of its political system and human rights record, most Americans believe relations with China are important to US interests and are in favor of engaging China diplomatically and economically.

NATIONAL PRIDE
Citizens' pride in their country
2003–04
20 = highest pride
0 = lowest pride

Americans are proud of their country in general terms, and the more proud individuals are, the more likely they are to take a nationalistic approach to foreign affairs, with men scoring more highly than women in this respect. Americans also take more pride than any other nation in their country's history, influence in the world, armed forces, economic, scientific, and technological achievements, its fair and equal treatment of all groups in society, and in its democratic principles.

Venezuela 13.4, USA 12.7, Australia 12.5, South Africa 12.0, Canada 12.0, Philippines 11.7, Russia 11.7, Spain 11.5, Israel 11.2, South Korea 11.0, Japan 10.9, Poland 10.3, UK 10.1, France 9.4

VIEWS OF OTHERS
Approval rating by Americans of selected countries *2006*
50 = very favorable
0 = neutral
–50 = very unfavorable

The approval ratings Americans give to other countries reflect similarities of policy and world view, and appreciation of those who support their country's foreign policy.

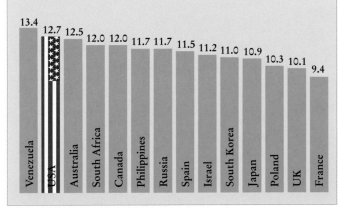

UK 21, Australia 19, Japan 8, Germany 7, Israel 4, –3 Mexico, –3 France, –4 India, –6 South Korea, –9 Indonesia, –10 China, –16 Saudi Arabia, –23 Iraq, –27 North Korea, –29 Iran

HOW THE WORLD SEES AMERICA

Since the 2003 invasion of Iraq, America's image has declined and its favorability ratings trail those of other major countries.

Immediately after the events of 9/11 Americans benefited from a period of sympathy from around the world. This soon dissipated, however, as people came to see the reaction of the USA as excessive, with the War on Terror drawing majority support in very few countries.

Negative attitudes towards the USA are widespread; they exist in several countries in Europe, most Muslim countries, and parts of the Far East, notably China. A majority of people in many countries take a negative view of America's military supremacy, and in most countries a large majority supports the emergence of a competing military superpower. Muslim countries are especially concerned that American military power is a threat to them.

Negative attitudes focus more on US government policy and

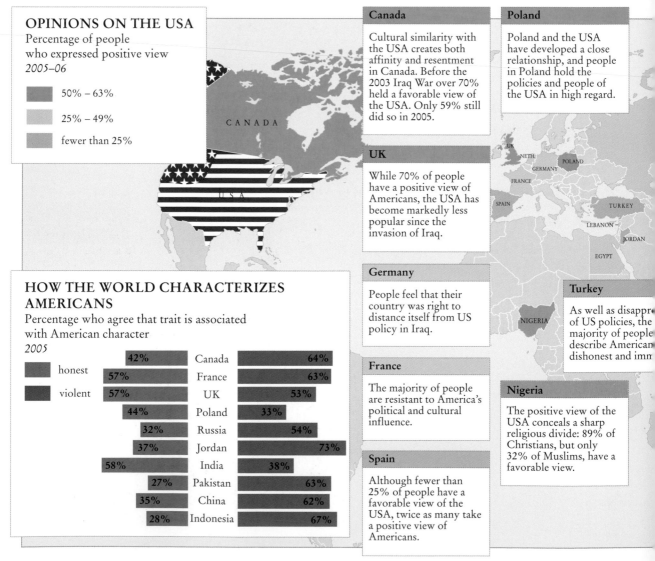

OPINIONS ON THE USA
Percentage of people who expressed positive view
2005–06

- 50% – 63%
- 25% – 49%
- fewer than 25%

HOW THE WORLD CHARACTERIZES AMERICANS
Percentage who agree that trait is associated with American character
2005

- honest
- violent

Country	honest	violent
Canada	42%	64%
France	57%	63%
UK	57%	53%
Poland	44%	33%
Russia	32%	54%
Jordan	37%	73%
India	58%	38%
Pakistan	27%	63%
China	35%	62%
Indonesia	28%	67%

Canada
Cultural similarity with the USA creates both affinity and resentment in Canada. Before the 2003 Iraq War over 70% held a favorable view of the USA. Only 59% still did so in 2005.

UK
While 70% of people have a positive view of Americans, the USA has become markedly less popular since the invasion of Iraq.

Germany
People feel that their country was right to distance itself from US policy in Iraq.

France
The majority of people are resistant to America's political and cultural influence.

Spain
Although fewer than 25% of people have a favorable view of the USA, twice as many take a positive view of Americans.

Poland
Poland and the USA have developed a close relationship, and people in Poland hold the policies and people of the USA in high regard.

Turkey
As well as disapprov of US policies, the majority of people describe American dishonest and imm

Nigeria
The positive view of the USA conceals a sharp religious divide: 89% of Christians, but only 32% of Muslims, have a favorable view.

leadership rather than on the American people, who are held in higher esteem than their government by the rest of the world. Americans are generally respected as being hardworking and inventive, and admired for their wealth, but only in a minority of countries are they seen as honest and moral. A deeply unflattering picture of Americans as greedy, violent, insular, insensitive, and rude emerges among public opinion in a wide range of countries, with the most negative attitudes apparent in Muslim countries.

It is perhaps not surprising, then, that in most countries, the exception being India, America is no longer seen as a land of opportunity, an accolade that it has ceded mainly to other English-speaking countries such as Australia and Canada.

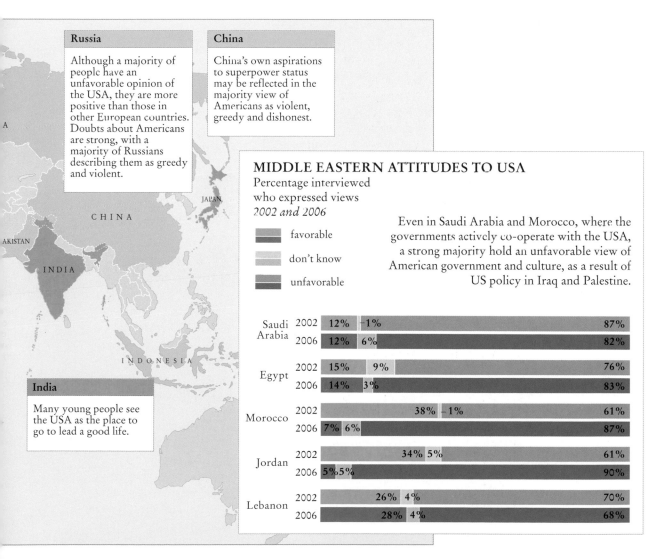

Russia

Although a majority of people have an unfavorable opinion of the USA, they are more positive than those in other European countries. Doubts about Americans are strong, with a majority of Russians describing them as greedy and violent.

China

China's own aspirations to superpower status may be reflected in the majority view of Americans as violent, greedy and dishonest.

India

Many young people see the USA as the place to go to lead a good life.

MIDDLE EASTERN ATTITUDES TO USA

Percentage interviewed who expressed views
2002 and 2006

- favorable
- don't know
- unfavorable

Even in Saudi Arabia and Morocco, where the governments actively co-operate with the USA, a strong majority hold an unfavorable view of American government and culture, as a result of US policy in Iraq and Palestine.

		favorable	don't know	unfavorable
Saudi Arabia	2002	12%	1%	87%
	2006	12%	6%	82%
Egypt	2002	15%	9%	76%
	2006	14%	3%	83%
Morocco	2002	38%	1%	61%
	2006	7%	6%	87%
Jordan	2002	34%	5%	61%
	2006	5%	5%	90%
Lebanon	2002	26%	4%	70%
	2006	28%	4%	68%

DIPLOMACY AND INTELLIGENCE

America spends money on trying to create a favorable impression abroad of its culture and policies, and on discovering the hidden intentions behind the policies of its potential adversaries.

In its public diplomacy the US government seeks to shape the environment overseas by influencing public opinion in other countries so as to promote its own national interest and national security. It recognizes the importance of speaking directly to citizens of other countries, and in 2005 the USA spent more than $1.5 billion on activities designed to improve its message to people across the world. All major embassies now have programs of public diplomacy as part of their brief. The growth of anti-Americanism since 2003 has put a premium on the use of public diplomacy to combat the negative image of America that has become so prevalent.

The US intelligence community consists of 16 intelligence-gathering organizations. After the failure to give adequate warning of 9/11, the Commission investigating the attack questioned the

PUBLIC DIPLOMACY

Diplomacy as propaganda
Public diplomacy is often associated with propaganda, which carries connotations of manipulation and deceit. If the information disseminated to win people over to a more favorable view of America is based on fact, then it might be considered benign. If it is based on falsehood, then it is more accurately described as disinformation. The USA has been widely accused of funding magazines, planting articles in the foreign press, and influencing journalists for this purpose.

Cultural diplomacy
American art, dance, film, jazz, and literature continue to inspire people the world over. Projecting American culture through, for example, government-sponsored tours by dance companies or orchestras of developing countries, is an effective way of communicating with young people, many of whom still admire American culture and values, even if they resent and reject US government policy.

But the fact that these tours *are* government funded undermines their credibility. Privately owned news and cultural organizations, while profit-making, at least have the advantage of being able to distance themselves from government policies.

America and Islam
The most difficult task for pubic diplomacy is to confront the collapse of trust in America in the Islamic world. The root of Muslim disaffection is US Middle East policy. Increasingly, among Arabs, the traditional differentiation between views of Americans and of American policy is collapsing. Beneath this lies the feeling that America lacks understanding of, and respect for, Islamic civilization.

Arabs see the root of this lack of understanding in the belief by most Americans that people from other nations, including Arabs, aspire to emulate American culture. The inability of many Americans to imagine that Arabs might hold different values allows America to engage, in the name of freedom and democracy, on a crusade to change the Arab world to reflect its own values.

The apparent lack of concern among the American public for the scale of Arab casualties in the Middle East conflict, compared with their preoccupation with American casualties, demonstrates to Arab opinion an unacceptable double standard. The US government has increased the public diplomacy budget for, and redeployed staff in, Muslim countries, with a view to marginalizing extremists, although still only 30 percent of diplomats serving in Muslim countries have requisite language skills.

effectiveness of the intelligence community in protecting US security. It identified a lack of co-operation and co-ordination among the agencies, and recommended the creation of a Director of National Intelligence to oversee the community, a task made more urgent by failures of intelligence in the Iraq war. The size and cost of the intelligence community is treated as classified information, but the total budget was disclosed in 1997 and 1998, when it stood at nearly $27 billion. The intelligence community is so large and diverse that it remains unclear whether the reorganization can make it effective. And yet its importance is demonstrated by the scale of the consequences of its failures; in the face of the perceived threat from terrorism the response will be to enhance America's intelligence capability rather than reduce it.

> " WHAT THE ENEMIES OF THE **USA** HOPE TO DENY, WE WORK TO REVEAL. "
>
> GEORGE J. TENET
> FORMER DIRECTOR OF
> CENTRAL INTELLIGENCE
> FEBRUARY 2004

SECRET INTELLIGENCE

National Security Agency (NSA)

The NSA is the largest intelligence-gathering organization in the world. It exists to protect US secrets and to discover those of others. It is part of the Department of Defense and aims to dominate global cryptology as effectively as the US armed forces dominate conventional military power. In addition to military and diplomatic code breaking it has, in conjunction with its counterparts in allied countries, the capacity to monitor a large proportion of the world's transmitted civilian telephone, fax, and data traffic. This creates fears that, under the cloak of secrecy, justified by the threat to security, it has become an eavesdropping agency involved in industrial and political espionage, which violates the privacy of US citizens – even within the USA, where its charter prohibits it from

operating. Its size remains unknown, but on its own admission, if the NSA were considered a corporation in terms of dollars spent, floor space occupied, and personnel employed, it would rank in the top 10 percent of the Fortune 500 companies.

Central Intelligence Agency (CIA)

The primary purpose of the CIA is to obtain and analyze information about foreign governments, corporations, and individuals, and report this information to other branches of government. It produces studies on topics of interest to national security policymakers, often based on intelligence acquired from human sources. It is also a propaganda agency, which uses covert means to disseminate information that promotes US interests.

The CIA also has an operational aspect through which it influences political, economic, or military conditions abroad at the request of the President, but in a way that conceals the US role. This has, in the eyes of many, given it a mythically powerful role in shaping the world. While the CIA has certainly intervened in the affairs of other countries, notably in funding mujahadeen guerrillas in Afghanistan in their fight against the Soviet Union in the 1980s – a decision that has since come to haunt it – its well-known failures as a provider of intelligence estimates must cast doubt on its effectiveness out of the public eye. These failures have reduced its standing and it is one of the losers in the Washington competition between intelligence agencies.

CULTURE WARS

Americans have created a global culture that reflects their values and way of life, but other cultures are fighting back.

Globalization has brought about the standardization of consumer products, and brands such as McDonald's and Coca-Cola project American consumer culture across the world. Similarly, movies, books, and photos now circle the globe in an instant, via satellite television and the internet, and American corporations such as Time Warner (CNN), News Corporation (Fox, Star), Viacom (MTV), Microsoft, and Google are prominent. The US entertainment industry measures its annual export revenue in tens of billions of dollars, and the US government takes a strong line in protecting the intellectual property rights on which the industry depends.

Communication is double-edged, however, and US hypocrisy is often exposed by the global communications it has helped develop. In many parts of the world, the media projects an image of the USA as uncivilized, uncouth, and unlettered. Movies and television are two main conduits of American popular culture, but are quite widely disliked even among people who have a favorable view of the USA.

English owes its world presence to the USA, and its spread has facilitated the projection of American culture and ideas. While Mandarin Chinese is spoken by more people than any other language, between a quarter and a third of the world's people speak English with some competence. Many more use English as a second language, and it has official status in over 75 countries. The media and internet has a predominantly English voice, but there has also been a growth of blended languages: Spanglish in the USA, Taglish in the Philippines, and Inglish in India. This embeds American ideas and values in other cultures, even as the language is adapted to their needs. Its combination of flexibility and pervasiveness makes English the perfect conduit for the projection of American soft power.

THE LANGUAGE OF THE WEB
Languages' share of internet use
2006

- Arabic 3%
- Italian 3%
- Korean 3%
- Portuguese 3%
- French 5%
- German 5%
- Spanish 8%
- Japanese 8%
- Chinese 14%
- English 30%
- rest of world 18%

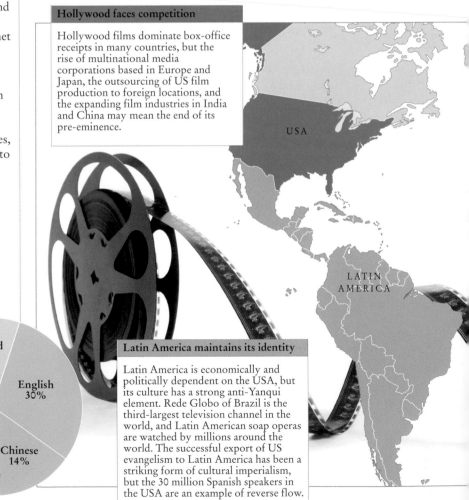

Hollywood faces competition

Hollywood films dominate box-office receipts in many countries, but the rise of multinational media corporations based in Europe and Japan, the outsourcing of US film production to foreign locations, and the expanding film industries in India and China may mean the end of its pre-eminence.

USA

LATIN AMERICA

Latin America maintains its identity

Latin America is economically and politically dependent on the USA, but its culture has a strong anti-Yanqui element. Rede Globo of Brazil is the third-largest television channel in the world, and Latin American soap operas are watched by millions around the world. The successful export of US evangelism to Latin America has been a striking form of cultural imperialism, but the 30 million Spanish speakers in the USA are an example of reverse flow.

Nor are American media conglomerates any longer the unchallenged champions of cultural globalization, with new media corporations developing in competition with US giants.

Unlike wheat or coal, cultural products are intimately bound up with social identity. Conflict, therefore, is to be expected as new influences come up against well-grounded traditions. Other cultures have a strong sense of their own values and will not simply capitulate to American-inspired alternatives. So, while there is adaptation and a fusion of new and old cultures, there is also resistance to American influence as other cultures defend themselves.

France stands up to USA

The French have long sought to protect their national identity from other cultures, and have recently launched a worldwide News Channel, France 24. Branches of McDonald's in France have been subject to arson attacks, and the government has attempted to restrict the number of US films shown in French cinema and on television. Mutual antipathy reached a peak after the invasion of Iraq, with boycotts of consumer goods and Americans renaming French fries "freedom fries".

Taliban *v* American values

The US conflict with the Taliban in Afghanistan is fundamentally cultural, with a sense of Christian mission driving US policy, and the traditional Qur'anic schools, or Madrassas, supplying Taliban fighters. The different perspectives on the role of women in society show how far apart the two cultures are. The strongly ideological character of the conflict makes it virtually irreconcilable, as the continued fighting between a resurgent Taliban and NATO forces demonstrates.

China fights back

China is a growing market for western cultural exports, but its fear of foreign cultural influence is evident in the quota it has placed on imported films, and restrictions on satellite broadcasting and the internet. China itself has an effective soft-power diplomacy, cultivating relationships across Asia. It is winning influence by educating future elites from many Asian countries at its universities, and by showing more respect for Asian traditions than the USA has done.

Arab broadcasting networks

Resentment about the USA's treatment of Arabs is expressed through the broadcasting network Al Jazeera, the most widely watched TV network in the Arab world, based in Qatar. The US government has launched a competing Arab-language satellite TV station, Al Hurra, but it has had little success in overcoming antipathy to its Middle East policy. In a move that increases the competition for world opinion, Al Jazeera has launched an English-language TV network that will broadcast from Europe, Asia and the USA, as well as the Middle East.

India holds its own

Bollywood produces twice as many films as Hollywood, and its influence is spreading, with its overseas market accounting for up to a third of revenues. Outsourced film production may enable the Indian film industry to rival Hollywood. Call centers, another form of outsourcing, can lead to cultural tension, as captured in an Indian sitcom that portrays Americans as rude, arrogant, and racist when directed to an Indian call center.

Chapter Nine
THE FUTURE

The contribution of the USA to shaping the world order during the second half of the 20th century is hard to overestimate, but no empire lasts forever and American power may have passed its zenith. US pre-eminence faces a more complex combination of challenges than ever before. The events in Iraq since 2003 have undermined US credibility and may prompt a period of retrenchment. Over the longer term, however, environmental change and globalization are likely to have the greatest impact on the distribution of global power. The USA consumes energy at unsustainable rates and faces the prospect of being overtaken by Asia as the economic powerhouse of the world economy. The USA's determination to retain military superiority may also overtax its economy and create a gap between its ambitions and its capabilities. Its military superiority rests on technological superiority, but this may be eroded as nuclear and bio-chemical technologies become more widely accessible. An added danger is that the proliferation of weapons of mass destruction will be allied to the challenge of terrorism, which expresses in extreme form the backlash of the relatively powerless.

It is natural that, as the era of globalization settles into a more multi-polar formation, there should be popular resistance to US power and the attractions of its popular culture. The IMF, the UN Security Council, and other international organizations will evolve to reflect this. Of more concern to the USA is whether other nation states join together in new economic and security formations that exclude the USA. It cannot preserve its power by resisting these trends and meeting every challenge with force. Americans do not have the will for such crude imperialism. The USA must accommodate the changes, balancing national interests against global responsibilities. Consolidation of power requires willingness to serve the international system by creating consensus, rather than by attempting to impose solutions. The USA remains the only candidate for such a role, but fulfilling it will depend on sensitive leadership, not the exercise of raw power.

> " WE KNOW, THERE ARE KNOWN KNOWNS…WE ALSO KNOW THERE ARE KNOWN UNKNOWNS…BUT THERE ARE ALSO UNKNOWN UNKNOWNS – THE ONES WE DON'T KNOW WE DON'T KNOW. "
>
> DONALD RUMSFELD
> US SECRETARY OF DEFENSE
> 2003

The conduct of the USA in its battle with terrorism has weakened its international support and done little to improve its security.

The War on Terror is the US-led campaign to eliminate the threat of international terrorism. The war has spread beyond its original focus, and the USA now sees itself as leading the fight against a global phenomenon of terror, in collaboration with other states.

The War on Terror was launched in direct response to the events of September 11, 2001, and focused on militant Islamist groups such as Al Qaeda, on state sponsorship of terrorism, and on spreading the so-called freedom agenda. It does have diplomatic and financial aspects, but has largely been a military enterprise, the leading episodes being the overthrow of the Taliban in Afghanistan, and of Saddam Hussein in Iraq.

9/11 produced a global wave of sympathy for the USA, but belief that the administration of George W. Bush used the terrorist threat to justify an expansionist foreign policy has led to a loss of support in most countries. Iraq was presented by the USA as a rogue state, brutal towards its own people, bent on the acquisition of weapons of mass

Axis of Evil

The term was coined by President George W. Bush in his 2002 State of the Union speech to characterize states that sponsor terrorism. He named Iran, Iraq, and North Korea. In 2002, John R. Bolton, then Under Secretary of State, added Cuba, Syria, and Libya.

Sponsorship of terror by these states has not been established, and they are not sufficiently unified to form a basis for concerted action. Naming them in dramatic, religiously inspired terms did, however, galvanize American public opinion in favor of the war and justified aggressive policies against these states.

Patriot Act

Signed in October 2001, and renewed in 2006, the Act dramatically expanded the surveillance and investigative powers of law enforcement agencies. It created the offence of domestic terrorism and has been seen as attack on civil liberties in the USA, in particular on those of immigrants.

Guantánamo, Cuba

The detainment camp at the US naval base has held approximately 800 suspects without proper trial since 2002. The USA denies torture, but the camp has been the focus of worldwide criticism of US disregard for human rights and contempt for the rule of law.

CHANGING SUPPORT

Percentage of people who expressed support for US-led War on Terror
2002 and 2006

	2002	2006
Russia	73%	52%
UK	69%	49%
Japan	61%	39%
Indonesia	31%	30%
Pakistan	20%	26%

KEY LOCATIONS IN THE WAR ON TERROR
2000–06

- "axis of evil" as defined by the USA
- targets of terrorist attacks
- other countries
- countries alleged to have colluded with USA in practice of extraordinary rendition

USA
CUBA
COLOMBIA
PERU
ARGENTINA

destruction (WMDs), and in league with terrorist groups. In the event, only the first allegation was proved. Following the 2003 invasion, Iraq deteriorated into chaos, and has indeed become the central front in the War on Terror.

So is the USA winning the war? The majority of the world's 1.5 billion Muslims are now hostile to the USA, and Al Qaeda continues to recruit. And although America accepts that the war will be long, it does not have the domestic support for a sustained conflict, whereas its opponents think in terms of generations. Furthermore, the USA's marked disregard of human rights – routinely pursuing acts it would condemn in others – has made its proclaimed purpose of spreading the freedom agenda appear hypocritical.

In declaring the War on Terror, America devised rules by which only it plays. It has failed to recognize that the best antidote to terrorism is to uphold human dignity. By revealing its imperial mentality it has lost its moral credibility.

Extraordinary Rendition

Rendition is the practice of transferring individuals between countries without judicial process. It is used by the CIA to abduct suspects on foreign soil, or to receive them from foreign governments. Detainees are transferred to other states to be interrogated in ways not permissible under US law, which includes the use of torture.

Victims have been held in US-run secret detention centers outside US territory. The US administration has acknowledged the existence of these so-called "black sites", but denies torture, and contends that rendition is done in accordance with US law and treaty obligations.

The secrecy surrounding rendition makes its scale difficult to estimate. Although the threat of terrorism is real, the disregard for law and natural justice that the USA displays by these practices undermines its moral authority.

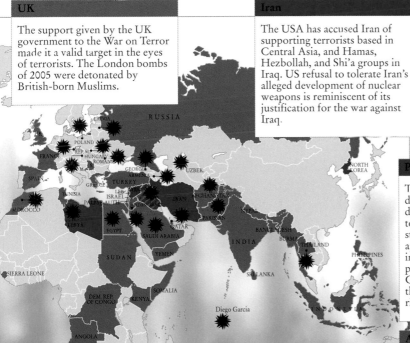

UK

The support given by the UK government to the War on Terror made it a valid target in the eyes of terrorists. The London bombs of 2005 were detonated by British-born Muslims.

Iran

The USA has accused Iran of supporting terrorists based in Central Asia, and Hamas, Hezbollah, and Shi'a groups in Iraq. US refusal to tolerate Iran's alleged development of nuclear weapons is reminiscent of its justification for the war against Iraq.

Post-invasion Iraq

The inability of the USA to demonstrate that Saddam had developed WMDs, and its failure to provide a viable post-invasion strategy, has made the USA appear duplicitous and incompetent. The treatment of prisoners in US custody at Abu Ghraib revealed the hypocrisy of their claim to be defending human rights.

Somalia

As Muslims gained control of much of Somalia in 2006, US concerns that it is a haven for Al Qaeda increased. The USA's bombing, in 2007, of sites suspected of sheltering terrorists demonstrated its willingness to act unilaterally.

Indonesia

Although the 2002 Bali bombing did not directly target Americans, the USA has provided support to the Indonesian government, which it regards as a key ally in the war on terror.

Afghanistan/Pakistan

The USA achieved a swift victory against the Taliban in 2001, but despite a continuing US military presence, the Taliban control large areas. Pakistan supports the USA in the War on Terror, but the Taliban and Al Qaeda continue to operate in the Afghan–Pakistan border region.

Global discontent with America has been clearly demonstrated, but has yet to coalesce into a coherent challenge to its power.

The unilateral and forceful character of US foreign policy since the late 1990s has been met with increasing resistance from individuals and groups. This has taken many forms – peaceful and violent, spontaneous and organized – and has touched every region of the world.

In 1999, the Global Justice Movement, a loose alliance of campaigners against globalization, demonstrated at the World Trade Organization (WTO) meeting in Seattle, and clashed with police. They attracted attention to the power of international economic institutions and America's role in them. Subsequent WTO meetings and those of the G8 leaders have been the focus of similar protests. The level of security now routinely required to insulate democratic leaders from the protestors is evidence of a breakdown of trust.

In countries where US foreign policy meets the strongest opposition, both governmental and non-governmental channels are employed. The regimes of Fidel Castro of Cuba and Hugo Chavez of Venezuela demonstrate government resistance to US power. Their survival, despite US attempts to undermine their position, shows that alternatives are possible even in America's own back yard. Even the government of

ANTI-WAR PROTESTS

A series of marches involving millions of people protesting the US invasion of Iraq has taken place around the world annually since immediately before the start of the war in March 2003. Although a powerful symbol of disenchantment with US government policies, it has had no immediate impact on those policies.

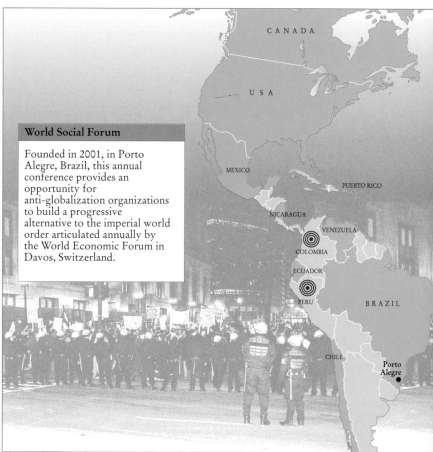

World Social Forum

Founded in 2001, in Porto Alegre, Brazil, this annual conference provides an opportunity for anti-globalization organizations to build a progressive alternative to the imperial world order articulated annually by the World Economic Forum in Davos, Switzerland.

Mexico, which maintains close economic ties with the USA, has been forced to grant concessions to the Zapatista Army of National Liberation, a guerrilla group opposed to the North American Free Trade Area (NAFTA).

America's close association with Israel has led to strong anti-American feelings among many Arabs. Hamas, the majority organization in the Palestinian National Authority, expresses its opposition through both its political and military wings. Hezbollah, a politico-military organization that controls much of southern Lebanon, effectively resisted Israel and, by proxy, America in the 2006 war. The USA lists the military wing of Hezbollah as a terrorist organization, while much of the Arab world supports it in its resistance struggle.

Terrorism is the most dramatic example of resistance, and, as demonstrated by the Madrid bombings of March 2004 and the London bombings of July 2005, it is not necessarily the result of a tightly organized group, but may be generated by a loose network of activists. In both cases, government support for the US-led invasion of Iraq, is thought to have been the justification for the attacks.

SITES OF RESISTANCE
2006

selected countries

 location of demonstrations against US intervention in Iraq, March 2006

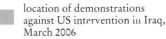 base of operation of foreign terrorist organizations, as designated by US Office of Counterterrorism

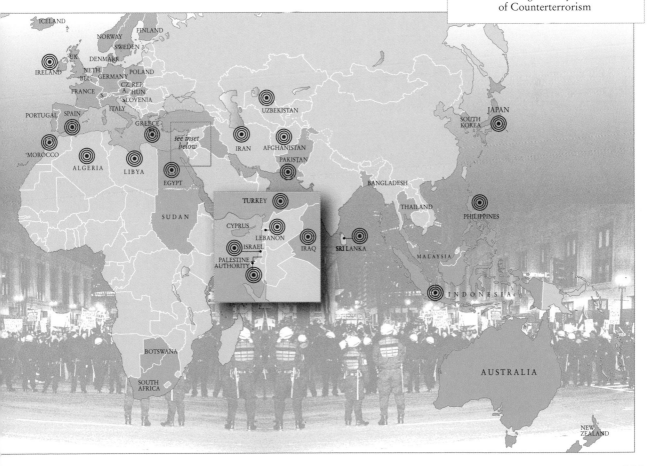

111

NECKLACE OR NOOSE

The USA faces the challenge of networks of other countries developing the potential to encircle it and combat its power.

The US national security strategy promises to maintain such an immense military power as to make its position impregnable. But other potential economic and military superpowers are beginning to emerge – Russia, from the chaos after the disintegration of the Soviet Union, India, with its enormous economic potential, and China, which is already laying the foundations for a leading world role. While none is yet in a sufficiently strong position to challenge the American empire, the question is can they combine to do so?

These emerging powers are building new connections that exclude the USA, and challenge the domination of the G7 countries. Latin America and Africa are included, alongside the emerging powers of Asia, with a thread of anti-Americanism running through many of these new alliances. However, there are competitive tensions between

Iran

Iran has agreed with India jointly to develop the world's largest gas field. It is also meeting a significant proportion of China's growing energy needs, and trade between the two countries grew by more than 40% in 2006. The two nations that pose the greatest challenge to American power are drawing together.

Opposition to the USA has provided the basis for closer relations with anti-imperialist countries in Latin America, including Nicaragua and Cuba. Iran and Venezuela are both leading members of OPEC and work together to exercise greater control of the world oil market.

European Union

The size and wealth of the EU make it a candidate for world leadership, its distinctive social democratic perspective contrasting with the harsher, market-oriented USA. However, a lack of internal coherence makes it unsuited to the role.

The EU has regular summits with the Caribbean and Latin America, but although both regions have an interest in moving away from reliance on the USA, they lack the internal unity to mount concerted action.

The EU engages with the Middle East peace process in an attempt to redress the pro-Israeli slant of US policy, but its impact is relatively minor.

The euro is a potential threat to the pre-eminence of the dollar as a reserve currency, on which much of America's wealth depends.

A pan-European alliance between the EU and Russia might shift the centre of gravity in world affairs, although strategic co-operation that would threaten US power is a long way off.

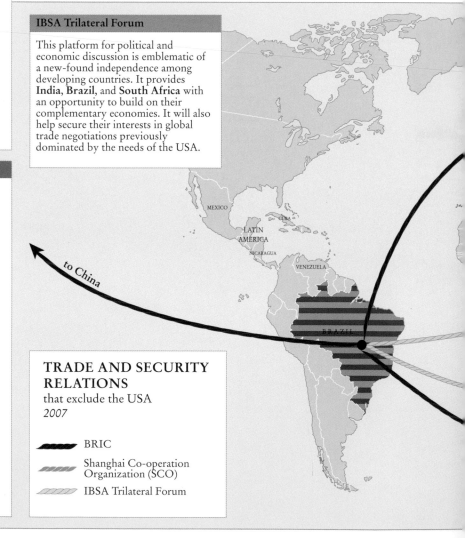

IBSA Trilateral Forum

This platform for political and economic discussion is emblematic of a new-found independence among developing countries. It provides **India**, **Brazil**, and **South Africa** with an opportunity to build on their complementary economies. It will also help secure their interests in global trade negotiations previously dominated by the needs of the USA.

to China

MEXICO
CUBA
LATIN AMERICA
NICARAGUA
VENEZUELA
BRAZIL

TRADE AND SECURITY RELATIONS
that exclude the USA
2007

━━━ BRIC

▨▨▨ Shanghai Co-operation Organization (SCO)

▨▨▨ IBSA Trilateral Forum

these new powers, enabling the USA to play them off against each other – a tactic that is a driving force of its foreign policy.

New networks are being driven by trade, with the World Trade Organization (WTO) providing a sufficiently flexible framework to incorporate the new powers without overturning the present order. The real challenge to the USA will be when the emerging powers develop political and security relationships. The USA has shown considerable flexibility in adapting to new patterns of trade, but has been rigid and confrontational on issues of security and natural resources. How well it adapts to this challenge will determine whether the emerging networks prove to be a necklace to adorn its power or a noose that will strangle it.

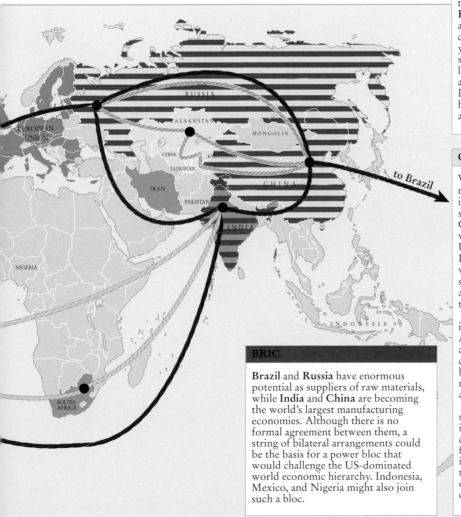

Shanghai Co-operation Organization (SCO)

This brings together **China**, **Russia**, and the Central Asian Republics of **Kazakhstan**, **Kyrgyzstan**, **Tajikistan**, and **Uzbekistan** to discuss security concerns in Central Asia. Although not yet a military bloc, and with mutual suspicion between Russia and China limiting its effectiveness, it is potentially a Eurasian equivalent of NATO. With Pakistan, India, Mongolia, and Iran having observer status, it could emerge as a wider anti-American bloc.

China

Will China become an antagonistic rival to the USA or be peacefully incorporated into the international system? Hungry for natural resources, China is establishing new partnerships with countries in Latin America – the USA's traditional sphere of influence. It has also developed close relations with Venezuela, which is hoping to supply 20% of China's oil imports in an attempt to reduce its dependence on the US market.

China is signing oil, gas, mining, infrastructure, and arms deals across Africa, offering investment and assistance with the minimum of conditions. Its hands-off approach to human rights is hindering poverty reduction and democratic accountability in Africa.

It is also translating its economic and military power into political influence in South-East Asia, leading the drive to create an East Asian Summit as a forum for security issues. While China increases its military relationships in the region, the USA is downgrading its own, and appears to be ceding regional dominance to China.

BRIC

Brazil and **Russia** have enormous potential as suppliers of raw materials, while **India** and **China** are becoming the world's largest manufacturing economies. Although there is no formal agreement between them, a string of bilateral arrangements could be the basis for a power bloc that would challenge the US-dominated world economic hierarchy. Indonesia, Mexico, and Nigeria might also join such a bloc.

SUSTAINING THE EMPIRE

So far this century, US foreign policy has failed to understand its own limitations or the rights of others. Unless America discovers a better balance, its empire will be short-lived.

The American achievement of creating a world order is impressive. The USA now presides over a network of international institutions, giving it a role in diplomacy, economics, and security which dwarfs that of any other country. Although it faces many challenges, and some vulnerabilities, including a large trade deficit and energy insecurity, the USA retains a pivotal role in world affairs. The question is whether this role is sustainable.

Expanding flows of information, technology, capital, goods, services, and people is the shaping force of all major trends for the foreseeable future, but it might well be slowed by a pandemic, terrorism, environmental disaster, energy shortage, or by inequality and social injustice. A combination of catastrophic events and inequality might also create a popular backlash. The USA has shaped globalization and will have to continue to be active if it is to preserve its superpower status as others try to reduce America's relative power.

Economic growth, expanding military capacity, and large populations will underpin the rise of Asia. This will offer an alternative to the market-dominated Washington consensus, bringing new attitudes to markets and to intervention, human rights, aid and culture, and may lead to Asianization replacing Americanization as the idea associated with globalization. However, the USA has long held the balance of power in Asia, and the potential for conflict in the region leaves it with a continuing, albeit less-decisive, role.

The USA is driven by fear that its global pre-eminence is only a window of opportunity, rather than a permanent position. It has tried to extend that window by developing unchallengeable military superiority, but faces the dual challenges of nuclear proliferation and terrorism. Its response has been a doctrine of pre-emptive intervention that breeds resentment and resistance. No country can yet rival US military power, but more will exact a heavy price for military action. To avoid this, the USA will have to use military power more judiciously.

New, intense lines of religious and cultural conflict are challenging the liberal ideology associated with the USA, with an increasingly politicized Islam emerging as a cross-national source of identity. By 2050, Muslims are expected to have grown from one-fifth to one-quarter of the world's population, whilst Christians will remain at one-third.

The overt Christianity of American culture is a fundamentalist counterpoint to its Islamic equivalent, and threatens to create, under the guise of a war on terror, a dangerous fault line in international affairs. Mutual understanding and respect is needed to prevent religious conflict dominating the first half of the 21st century.

The USA sees the spread of democratic government as key to peaceful co-operation, but while democracy has been extended in eastern Europe, its grip in Central Asia is tenuous, and China is little

INCREASE IN OIL IMPORT DEPENDENCY
Net US oil imports as percentage of total US supply
2000 and 2025

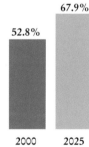

52.8%	67.9%
2000	2025

Energy insecurity is predicted to increase, and will continue to create US vulnerability. Some regions that could increase their oil output, such as the Caspian Sea, involve substantial political or economic risk for the USA. The pressure created by this competition for natural resources is likely to peak well before 2050. America will be put to the test in trying to protecting its own vulnerability while discharging a global responsibility for orderly change.

THE CHALLENGE OF SIZE

Global power is largely dependent on economic output. By 2050, the economic development of China and India, combined with their huge populations, will put their economies in the same league as that of the USA. The economic and cultural vitality of Japan and Russia will be adversely affected by declining and aging populations, as will that of the European Union, which faces a projected decline in working-age population of 52 million.

With both China and India well-placed to become technology leaders, the USA may struggle to retain its competitive and technological edge. Its task is to create a new international economic architecture that will maintain stability and growth, and can cope with the pressure points and crises that are bound to arise.

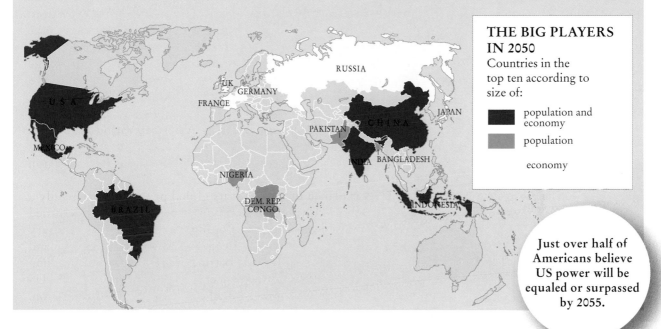

THE BIG PLAYERS IN 2050
Countries in the top ten according to size of:

- population and economy
- population
- economy

Just over half of Americans believe US power will be equaled or surpassed by 2055.

influenced by US conceptions of democracy. The USA has focused on the Middle East, with the intervention in Iraq seen as the first step to democratization across the region, but in practice it has contributed to a heightened Islamic consciousness that is more likely to result in a new Caliphate.

Over time, the sustainability of empire is inversely related to the use of force; empires rule best and longest through consent rather than by force of arms. In order to achieve a consensus that will extend its role in world affairs, the USA will have to retain its military power as a source of leadership, but it will also have to accept a greater degree of multilateralism, avoid direct confrontation, and practice indirect control by managing a balance of power than than by dictating one.

WORLD DATA TABLES

Countries	Population		Gross National Income (GNI) $ per capita 2005	Energy use million Btu per person 2004	CO$_2$ emissions million tonnes 2004
	thousands 2005 or latest available data	annual % growth 2005			
United States of America	296,497	0.96%	43,740	343	5,912.21
Afghanistan	–	–	–	1	0.69
Albania	3,130	0.58%	2,580	32	4.22
Algeria	32,854	1.52%	2,730	39	76.87
Angola	15,941	2.87%	1,350	12	19.74
Antigua and Barbuda	81	1.14%	10,920	115	0.55
Argentina	38,747	0.97%	4,470	71	142.25
Armenia	3,016	–0.32%	1,470	60	9.14
Australia	20,321	1.04%	32,220	264	386.18
Austria	8,211	0.47%	36,980	178	69.78
Azerbaijan	8,388	0.98%	1,240	83	36.78
Bahrain	727	1.50%	–	611	22.73
Bangladesh	141,822	1.86%	470	5	37.9
Barbados	270	0.25%	–	87	1.73
Belarus	9,776	–0.50%	2,760	94	55.3
Belgium	10,471	0.47%	35,700	269	147.64
Belize	292	3.20%	3,500	50	0.86
Benin	8,439	3.15%	510	4	2.02
Bhutan	918	2.42%	870	9	0.31
Bolivia	9,182	1.90%	1,010	23	11.26
Bosnia and Herzegovina	3,907	–0.06%	2,440	50	13.2
Botswana	1,765	–0.23%	5,180	33	3.83
Brazil	186,405	1.35%	3,460	49	336.71
Brunei	374	2.20%	–	274	5.68
Bulgaria	7,741	–0.26%	3,450	113	47.13
Burkina Faso	13,228	3.12%	400	1	1.15
Burma	50,519	1.03%	–	4	11.43
Burundi	7,548	3.58%	100	1	0.44
Cambodia	14,071	1.96%	380	1	0.58
Cameroon	16,322	1.76%	1,010	5	6.51
Canada	32,271	0.92%	32,600	418	587.98
Cape Verde	507	2.32%	1,870	5	0.15
Central African Republic	4,038	1.29%	350	1	0.35
Chad	9,749	3.14%	400	0	0.21
Chile	16,295	1.06%	5,870	75	61.98
China	1,304,500	0.64%	1,740	46	4,707.28
Colombia	45,600	1.51%	2,290	28	55.25
Comoros	600	2.11%	640	2	0.11
Congo	3,999	2.94%	950	5	2.97
Congo, Dem. Rep.	57,549	2.99%	120	1	1.8
Cook Islands	21	–1.20%	9,100	41	0.06
Costa Rica	4,327	1.73%	4,590	47	6.1
Côte d'Ivoire	18,154	1.57%	840	6	5.8
Croatia	4,444	0.05%	8,060	86	21.6
Cuba	11,269	0.22%	–	41	33.93
Cyprus	835	1.13%	–	147	8.27
Czech Republic	10,196	–0.19%	10,710	173	112.41
Denmark	5,418	0.26%	47,390	160	55.55

Balance of trade with USA US$ millions 2005	Legal emigrants to USA thousands 2005	Military spending US$ per person 2004	Arms imports from USA US$ millions 2001–02	Land area sq km 2005	Countries
–	–	935.64	–	9,629,090	United States of America
–194	4,749	17.55	1.45	652,090	Afghanistan
19	5,947	15.86	5.5	28,750	Albania
9,193	1,115	57.48	0.01	2,381,740	Algeria
7,556	188	18.83		1,246,700	Angola
–185	440		0	440	Antigua and Barbuda
472	7,081	108.76	8.44	2,780,400	Argentina
–20	2,591	45.26	–	29,800	Armenia
–8,430	3,193	566.95	155.76	7,741,220	Australia
3,507	532	182.90	7.08	83,870	Austria
–87	1,523	15.29	–	86,600	Azerbaijan
81	140	764.44	84.36	710	Bahrain
2,374	11,487	3.87	8.94	144,000	Bangladesh
–361	846		0.02	430	Barbados
310	3,503	17.10	–	207,600	Belarus
–5,589	859	296.89	68.77	32,545	Belgium
–119	876	27.39	0.13	22,970	Belize
–70	193	10.56	0.34	112,620	Benin
–2	30	4.17	–	47,000	Bhutan
75	2,197	16.60	1.03	1,098,580	Bolivia
53	14,074	52.89	4.62	51,210	Bosnia and Herzegovina
111	54	126.40	0.28	581,730	Botswana
9,091	16,664	72.04	39.26	8,514,880	Brazil
513	49	885.43	0.02	5,770	Brunei
186	5,635	47.79	1.57	110,990	Bulgaria
–23	128	3.40	–	274,000	Burkina Faso
–5	2,095	0.83	–	676,580	Burma
–3	186	5.40	–	27,830	Burundi
1,697	4,022	8.21	0.15	181,040	Cambodia
41	1,458	6.98	0	475,440	Cameroon
76,450	21,878	239.63	88.13	9,984,670	Canada
–7	1,225	22.24	0.38	4,030	Cape Verde
–9	24	3.17	0	622,980	Central African Republic
1,441	31	4.22	0.47	1,284,000	Chad
1,468	2,404	156.44	1.73	756,630	Chile
201,626	69,967	42.80	30.12	9,598,060	China
3,431	25,571	76.83	–	1,138,910	Colombia
1	–	8.94	–	2,230	Comoros
1,521	1,064		–	342,000	Congo
197	260	4.11	–	2,344,860	Congo, Dem. Rep.
0	–	–	–	237	Cook Islands
–177	2,278	17.18	0.2	51,100	Costa Rica
1,074	930	8.30	–	322,460	Côte d'Ivoire
205	1,780	115.66	0.1	56,540	Croatia
–361	36,261		–	110,860	Cuba
–53	196	492.22	–	9,250	Cyprus
1,158	476	116.22	4.45	78,870	Czech Republic
3,229	718	454.71	23.13	43,090	Denmark

119

Countries	Population		Gross National Income (GNI) $ per capita 2005	Energy use million Btu per person 2004	CO$_2$ emissions million tonnes 2004
	thousands 2005 or latest available data	annual % growth 2005			
Djibouti	793	1.78%	1,020	56	1.94
Dominica	72	0.75%	3,790	30	0.12
Dominican Republic	8,895	1.44%	2,370	34	20.3
East Timor	976	5.36%	750	–	–
Ecuador	13,228	1.43%	2,630	29	22.58
Egypt	74,033	1.90%	1,250	33	147.35
El Salvador	6,881	1.74%	2,450	19	6.13
Equatorial Guinea	504	2.27%	–	12	3.83
Eritrea	4,401	3.93%	220	2	0.82
Estonia	1,345	−0.30%	9,100	166	18.23
Ethiopia	71,256	1.83%	160	1	4.37
Fiji	848	0.82%	3,280	32	1.47
Finland	5,245	0.32%	37,460	258	61.48
France	60,743	0.60%	34,810	186	405.66
Gabon	1,384	1.57%	5,010	29	4.96
Gambia	1,517	2.63%	290	3	0.29
Georgia	4,474	−0.97%	1,350	30	4.22
Germany	82,485	−0.04%	34,580	178	862.23
Ghana	22,113	2.05%	450	7	6.25
Greece	11,089	0.29%	19,670	136	106.13
Grenada	107	0.71%	3,920	40	0.24
Guam	170	1.70%	15,000	207	2.51
Guatemala	12,599	2.44%	2,400	15	10.68
Guinea	9,402	2.15%	370	2	1.33
Guinea–Bissau	1,586	2.98%	180	4	0.38
Guyana	751	0.13%	1,010	31	1.72
Haiti	8,528	1.43%	450	3	1.7
Honduras	7,205	2.19%	1,190	14	6.04
Hungary	10,088	−0.19%	10,030	106	56.38
Iceland	295	1.03%	46,320	503	3.56
India	1,094,583	1.37%	720	14	1,112.84
Indonesia	220,558	1.36%	1,280	20	307.68
Iran	67,700	1.03%	2,770	96	401.91
Iraq	–	–	–	48	84
Ireland	4,151	2.00%	40,150	161	42.45
Israel	6,909	1.62%	18,620	141	66.24
Italy	57,471	−0.18%	30,010	142	484.98
Jamaica	2,657	0.48%	3,400	58	11.61
Japan	127,956	0.15%	38,980	178	1,262.10
Jordan	5,411	2.56%	2,500	50	18.65
Kazakhstan	15,146	0.88%	2,930	154	172.29
Kenya	34,256	2.33%	530	5	8.51
Kiribati	99	1.21%	1,390	4	0.03
Korea (North)	22,488	0.46%	–	39	69.35
Korea (South)	48,294	0.44%	15,830	186	496.76
Kuwait	2,535	3.04%	–	470	69.72
Kyrgyzstan	5,156	1.23%	440	33	3.7
Laos	5,924	2.26%	440	8	1.07

Balance of trade with USA US$ millions 2005	Legal emigrants to USA thousands 2005	Military spending US$ per person 2004	Arms imports from USA US$ millions 2001–02	Land area sq km 2005	Countries
−47	50	55.65	0.06	23,200	Djibouti
−58	198	–	0.01	750	Dominica
−105	27,504	19.89	0.9	48,730	Dominican Republic
−9		4.23	–	14,870	East Timor
3,779	11,608	53.88	1.67	283,560	Ecuador
−1,078	7,905	52.13	1,977.28	1,001,450	Egypt
143	21,359	16.70	1.63	21,040	El Salvador
1,313	10	56.71	–	28,050	Equatorial Guinea
−30	796	20.50	–	117,600	Eritrea
366	438	116.28	2.71	45,230	Estonia
−453	10,573	10.95	–	1,104,300	Ethiopia
141	1,422	43.89	–	18,270	Fiji
2,088	574	344.63	68.73	338,150	Finland
11,445	4,399	766.62	207.1	551,500	France
2,717	66	58.75	–	267,670	Gabon
−30	581	0.75	–	11,300	Gambia
−17	1,389	4.92	3.65	69,700	Georgia
50,663	9,264	470.70	222.26	357,030	Germany
−179	6,491	1.64	0.38	238,540	Ghana
−306	1,070	573.68	464.66	131,960	Greece
−77	840	–	0.12	340	Grenada
–	–			550	Guam
321	16,825	9.99	–	108,890	Guatemala
−50	495	16.29	0.55	245,860	Guinea
−2	26	3.96	–	36,120	Guinea–Bissau
−55	9,318	–	0.4	214,970	Guyana
−241	14,529	6.16	0.1	27,750	Haiti
506	7,012	4.88	1.96	112,090	Honduras
1,510	1,567	107.92	8.68	93,030	Hungary
−241	135	0.00	–	103,000	Iceland
10,849	84,681	10.66	0.04	3,287,260	India
8,971	3,924	4.13	14.12	1,904,570	Indonesia
79	13,887	142.61	–	1,648,200	Iran
7,666	4,077	49.86	–	438,320	Iraq
19,286	2,088	174.30	0.01	70,270	Ireland
7,143	5,755	1,429.03	696.78	22,140	Israel
19,496	3,066	347.66	103.68	301,340	Italy
−1,310	18,346	10.96	0.47	10,990	Jamaica
82,682	8,768	310.16	497.39	377,900	Japan
624	3,748	131.51	57.16	88,780	Jordan
563	2,229	14.61	3.04	2,724,900	Kazakhstan
−284	5,348	5.47	0.81	580,370	Kenya
−1	–	–	–	730	Kiribati
−6	–	227.72	–	120,540	Korea (North)
16,109	26,562	269.20	553.93	99,260	Korea (South)
2,361	1,152	842.17	132.73	17,820	Kuwait
−26	656	3.73	2.25	199,900	Kyrgyzstan
−6	1,242	8.85	0.1	236,800	Laos

Countries	Population		Gross National Income (GNI) $ per capita 2005	Energy use million Btu per person 2004	CO$_2$ emissions million tonnes 2004
	thousands 2005 or latest available data	annual % growth 2005			
Latvia	2,300	−0.55%	6,760	75	8.4
Lebanon	3,577	1.03%	6,180	63	16.4
Lesotho	1,795	−0.18%	960	3	0.21
Liberia	3,283	1.31%	130	3	0.52
Libya	5,853	1.95%	5,530	133	50.21
Lithuania	3,415	−0.60%	7,050	99	13.83
Luxembourg	457	0.75%	65,630	432	12.32
Macedonia	2,034	0.18%	2,830	55	7.64
Madagascar	18,606	2.69%	290	2	2.12
Malawi	12,884	2.16%	160	2	0.8
Malaysia	25,347	1.80%	4,960	107	153.64
Maldives	329	2.46%	2,390	45	1.1
Mali	13,518	2.96%	380	1	0.63
Malta	404	0.70%	13,590	104	3.07
Marshall Islands	63	3.29%	2,930	–	–
Mauritania	3,069	2.92%	560	17	3.27
Mauritius	1,248	1.11%	5,260	45	3.92
Mexico	103,089	1.01%	7,310	63	385.46
Micronesia, Fed. States	110	0.72%	2,300	–	–
Moldova	4,206	−0.29%	880	28	6.4
Mongolia	2,554	1.55%	690	34	8.17
Morocco	30,168	1.15%	1,730	14	29.23
Mozambique	19,792	1.88%	310	7	1.85
Namibia	2,031	1.09%	2,990	28	2.61
Nepal	27,133	2.02%	270	2	2.82
Netherlands	16,329	0.29%	36,620	251	266.99
New Caledonia	234	1.90%	–	131	1.9
New Zealand	4,110	1.20%	25,960	221	37.8
Nicaragua	5,487	2.04%	910	13	4.29
Niger	13,957	3.34%	240	1	1.24
Nigeria	131,530	2.17%	560	8	93.95
Norway	4,618	0.59%	59,590	424	51.14
Oman	2,567	1.30%	–	129	23.31
Pakistan	155,772	2.41%	690	12	106.27
Palau	20	1.00%	7,630	–	–
Palestine Authority	3,626	3.31%	–	–	–
Panama	3,232	1.75%	4,630	68	12.76
Papua New Guinea	5,887	1.98%	660	14	4.69
Paraguay	6,158	2.32%	1,280	68	3.85
Peru	27,968	1.46%	2,610	21	27.32
Philippines	83,054	1.75%	1,300	15	74.68
Poland	38,165	−0.04%	7,110	95	287.65
Portugal	10,557	0.52%	16,170	106	63.43
Puerto Rico	3,911	0.42%	–	141	39.31
Qatar	813	4.52%	–	840	38.86
Romania	21,632	−0.24%	3,830	74	95.29
Russia	143,151	−0.49%	4,460	209	1,684.84
Rwanda	9,038	1.73%	230	2	0.79

Balance of trade with USA US$ millions 2005	Legal emigrants to USA thousands 2005	Military spending US$ per person 2004	Arms imports from USA US$ millions 2001–02	Land area sq km 2005	Countries
185	769	37.99	1.7	64,590	Latvia
–377	4,282	141.40	3.18	10,400	Lebanon
400	12	16.74	0	30,350	Lesotho
16	4,880	2.69	–	111,370	Liberia
1,479	223	225.46	–	1,759,540	Libya
245	2,417	64.16	7.46	65,300	Lithuania
–394	35	315.43	2.42	–	Luxembourg
17	1,070	97.80	8.92	25,710	Macedonia
296	60	2.90	–	587,040	Madagascar
88	131	1.02	0	118,480	Malawi
23,252	2,632	70.55	12.13	329,740	Malaysia
–4	6	98.71	–	300	Maldives
–29	277	36.77	0.01	1,240,190	Mali
89	74	150.55	1	320	Malta
–70	32	–	–	180	Marshall Islands
–85	275	12.02	–	1,025,520	Mauritania
191	99	7.89	–	2,040	Mauritius
50,149	161,445	37.66	4.55	1,958,200	Mexico
–24	–	–	–	700	Micronesia, Fed. States
10	3,507	1.44	1.41	33,840	Moldova
122	323	8.28	0.11	1,566,500	Mongolia
–85	4,411	42.78	7.21	446,550	Morocco
–50	54	1.81	0	801,590	Mozambique
16	63	35.99	0.04	824,290	Namibia
86	3,158	2.07	0.06	147,180	Nepal
–11,634	1,815	396.17	242.58	41,530	Netherlands
–12	5	888.25	–	18,580	New Caledonia
508	1,293	150.11	32.17	270,530	New Zealand
561	3,305	4.76	–	130,000	Nicaragua
–16	126	1.69	0.02	1,267,000	Niger
22,573	10,598	3.25	3.76	923,770	Nigeria
4,880	423	677.77	88.78	323,760	Norway
–38	101	807.46	1.61	309,500	Oman
2,006	14,926	18.25	6.46	796,100	Pakistan
–12	8	–	–	–	Palau
1	–	–	–	–	Palestine Authority
–1,842	1,815	40.76	0.23	75,520	Panama
3	44	7.25	–	462,840	Papua New Guinea
–844	516	19.69	0.03	406,750	Paraguay
2,831	15,676	35.81	0.3	1,285,220	Peru
2,355	60,748	11.33	22.6	300,000	Philippines
680	15,352	90.77	31.6	312,690	Poland
1,199	1,125	121.71	28.85	91,980	Portugal
–	–	–	–	8,950	Puerto Rico
–538	174	837.73	0.83	11,000	Qatar
576	7,103	44.11	7.29	238,390	Romania
11,336	18,083	125.50–	–	17,098,240	Russia
–4	276	7.06	–	26,340	Rwanda

Countries	Population		Gross National Income (GNI) $ per capita 2005	Energy use million Btu per person 2004	CO$_2$ emissions million tonnes 2004
	thousands 2005 or latest available data	annual % growth 2005			
Saint Kitts and Nevis	48	2.14%	8,210	42	0.12
Saint Lucia	166	1.12%	4,800	34	0.39
Saint Vincent and the Grenadines	119	0.52%	3,590	27	0.19
Samoa	185	0.67%	2,090	14	0.15
São Tomé and Principe	157	2.30%	390	8	0.1
Saudi Arabia	24,573	2.57%	11,770	236	365.07
Senegal	11,658	2.36%	710	6	4.66
Serbia and Montenegro	8,168	0.26%	3,280	71	52.71
Seychelles	84	1.01%	8,290	148	0.87
Sierra Leone	5,525	3.48%	220	2	0.97
Singapore	4,351	2.59%	27,490	445	129.46
Slovakia	5,387	0.09%	7,950	147	38.45
Slovenia	1,998	0.06%	17,350	164	18.26
Solomon Islands	478	2.53%	590	5	0.19
Somalia	8,228	3.25%	–	1	0.75
South Africa	45,192	−0.70%	4,960	115	429.56
Spain	43,389	1.62%	25,360	159	361.9
Sri Lanka	19,582	0.84%	1,160	10	11.64
Sudan	36,233	1.98%	640	4	9.81
Suriname	449	0.62%	2,540	86	1.74
Swaziland	1,131	0.99%	2,280	18	1.34
Sweden	9,024	0.36%	41,060	258	59.07
Switzerland	7,441	0.69%	54,930	172	44.91
Syria	19,043	2.45%	1,380	46	52.88
Taiwan	23,036	0.61%	29,000	193	308
Tajikistan	6,507	1.19%	330	39	6.92
Tanzania	38,329	1.85%	340	2	3.53
Thailand	64,233	0.84%	2,750	54	218.59
Togo	6,145	2.58%	350	6	2.11
Tonga	102	0.32%	2,190	17	0.13
Trinidad and Tobago	1,305	0.30%	10,440	547	32.56
Tunisia	10,022	0.90%	2,890	33	20.81
Turkey	72,636	1.26%	4,710	51	211.69
Turkmenistan	4,833	1.40%	–	166	46.64
Uganda	28,816	3.52%	280	2	1.61
Ukraine	47,111	−0.72%	1,520	137	363.51
United Arab Emirates	4,533	4.82%	–	925	141.13
United Kingdom	60,203	0.56%	37,600	167	579.68
Uruguay	3,463	0.69%	4,360	51	5.84
Uzbekistan	26,593	1.45%	510	84	120.56
Vanuatu	211	1.93%	1,600	6	0.09
Venezuela	26,577	1.71%	4,810	115	142.68
Vietnam	82,966	0.97%	620	11	57.48
Virgin Islands (US)	115	1.63%	–	2,245	15.97
Yemen	20,975	3.12%	600	8	10.53
Zambia	11,668	1.64%	490	11	2.34
Zimbabwe	13,010	0.56%	340	17	11.88

Balance of trade with USA US$ millions 2005	Legal emigrants to USA thousands 2005	Military spending US$ per person 2004	Arms imports from USA US$ millions 2001–02	Land area sq km 2005	Countries
−44	342	–	0.01	360	Saint Kitts and Nevis
−102	832	–	–	620	Saint Lucia
−30	625	–	0.04	390	Saint Vincent and the Grenadines
−7	173	–	–	2,840	Samoa
−10	–	2.13	–	960	São Tomé and Principe
20,398	1,210	692.71	1,353.05	2,149,690	Saudi Arabia
−154	913	5.86	0.2	196,720	Senegal
−77	5,202	60.39	–	102,170	Serbia and Montenegro
-15	16	157.66	0.32	460	Seychelles
−28	2,731	1.75	-	71,740	Sierra Leone
−5,529	1,204	1,009.94	425	680	Singapore
811	965	74.76	4.22	49,030	Slovakia
178	114	183.99	0.55	20,270	Slovenia
−1	–	–	–	28,900	Solomon Islands
−9	5,829	1.99		637,660	Somalia
1,983	4,536	39.37	0.31	1,219,090	South Africa
1,683	1,888	213.18	178.16	505,370	Spain
1,885	1,894	35.83	–	65,610	Sri Lanka
−90	5,231	14.46	–	2,505,810	Sudan
−78	300	–	0.02	163,270	Suriname
187	16	17.57	–	17,360	Swaziland
10,118	1,517	488.23	57.42	450,290	Sweden
2,249	1,092	340.23	35.8	41,280	Switzerland
167	2,831	46.51	–	185,180	Syria
12,788	9,196	330.83	1,469.73	32,260	Taiwan
212	207	4.94	–	142,550	Tajikistan
- 63	829	0.54	0	945,090	Tanzania
12,659	5,505	27.65	170	513,120	Thailand
−21	1,523	4.39	–	56,790	Togo
−5	309	–	0.04	750	Tonga
6,441	6,568	83.72	0.13	5,130	Trinidad and Tobago
−30	495	35.34	6.33	163,610	Tunisia
903	4,614	116.28	282.39	783,560	Turkey
−102	148	18.17	–	488,100	Turkmenistan
−37	858	4.57	–	241,040	Uganda
571	22,761	13.15	7.85	603,700	Ukraine
−7,007	812	624.27	93.05	83,600	United Arab Emirates
12,435	19,800	524.48	251.5	243,610	United Kingdom
377	1,154	73.19	2.92	176,220	Uruguay
22	2,887	7.45	3.13	447,400	Uzbekistan
−7	–	–	–	12,190	Vanuatu
27,556	10,645	36.81	18.1	912,050	Venezuela
5,438	32,784	7.78	–	331,690	Vietnam
–	8	–	–	350	Virgin Islands (US)
61	3,366	23.28	0.31	527,970	Yemen
3	499	2.97	–	752,610	Zambia
50	923	51.4	0.02	390,760	Zimbabwe

DATA SOURCES

INTRODUCTION

16–17 AMERICA'S GLOBAL FOOTPRINT
AMERICANIZING THE GLOBE
<www.mcdonalds.com/corporate/investor/financialinfo/
financials/media/downloadablefinancials.xls> accessed 2003

Office of the United States Trade Representative:
<www.cfr.org/publication/10890/rise_in_bilateral_free_
trade_agreements.html#3> accessed February 2007
<www.c7f.navy.mil/Pages/Forwardpresence.html>
<www.c3f.navy.mil/mission_page.htm>
<edition.cnn.com/SPECIALS/2003/iraq/forces/coalition/
deployment/navy/5th.fleet.html>
<www.cusnc.navy.mil/Orders%20to%20Command/pages/
command.htm>
<www.answers.com/topic/united-states-6th-fleet>
<www.c6f.navy.mil> < navysite.de/navy/fleet.htm>
<en.wikipedia.org/wiki/United_States_Fleet_Forces_
Command>

World Federation of Exchanges: Focus no. 167, January
2007, page 31

ECOLOGICAL FOOTPRINT
<Global Footprint Network <www.footprintnetwork.org/
index.php>

GLOBAL WEALTH; SPENDING POWER
World Bank data statistics

Chapter One: ENERGY

20–21 ENERGY CONSUMPTION
ANNUAL ENERGY USE; ENERGY USE
Energy Information Administration
<www.eia.doe.gov> *International Energy Annual 2004*

22–23 ENERGY POLICY
US ENERGY SOURCES
Energy Information Administration
<www.eia.doe.gov> *Annual Review 2005*, Table 1.3

INCREASING ENERGY USE
Energy Information Administration, *Annual Review 2005*,
Table 1.5

US NUCLEAR ENERGY
Energy Information Administration, *Annual Review 2005*,
Table 9.2

NUCLEAR ENERGY WORLDWIDE
Energy Information Administration, *Annual Review 2005*,
Table 11.18

24–25 CLIMATE CHANGE
EMISSIONS AND INTENSITY
Energy Information Administration <www.eia.doe.gov>
Annual Review 2004, Table H.1

GREENHOUSE GASES
International Energy Agency Data Services
<data.iea.org/stats/eng/main.html>

TRANSPORT EMISSIONS
International Energy Agency Data Services
<data.iea.org/stats/eng/main.html>

26–27 ENERGY SECURITY
KNOWN OIL RESERVES WORLDWIDE
Bob Tiptree (ed), *International Petroleum Encyclopedia
2001*, PennWell Books, 2001

HOTSPOTS
Energy Information Administration <www.eia.doe.gov>
World Energy Hotspots

CHOKEPOINTS
Energy Information Administration
<www.eia.doe.gov> World Oil Transit Chokepoints

US OIL IMPORTS
Energy Information Administration Petroleum Navigator
<www.eia.doe.gov>

28–29 OIL: CONSUMPTION AND DEPENDENCY
US OIL IMPORTS
Energy Information Administration Petroleum Navigator
<www.eia.doe.gov>

INCREASING IMPORT DEPENDENCY
Energy Information Administration <www.eia.doe.gov>
Annual Energy Review 2005, Table 5.1

TOP OIL CONSUMERS
Energy Information Administration
<www.eia.doe.gov> *International Energy Annual 2004*
Table 3.5

30–31 OIL POLICY
FUTURE OIL IMPORTS
Energy Information Administration, *International Energy
Outlook 2006*, Chapter 3: World Oil Markets, Table 7
<www.eia.doe.gov/oiaf/ieo/oil.html>

Chapter Two: TRADE

34–35 IMBALANCE OF TRADE
US BALANCE OF TRADE
TradeStats Express. Presented by the Office of Trade and
Industry Information (OTII), Manufacturing and Services,
International Trade Administration, US Department of
Commerce <tse.export.gov>

US OVERALL BALANCE; US DEFICIT WITH CHINA
Bureau of Economic Analysis, International Economic
Accounts, Balance of Payments
<www.bea.gov/bea/di/home/bop.htm>

36–37 TRADING PARTNERS
US TRADE AGREEMENTS
Websites of featured organizations

VALUE OF US TRADE
TradeStats Express. Presented by the Office of Trade and
Industry Information (OTII), Manufacturing and Services,
International Trade Administration, US Department of
Commerce <tse.export.gov>

38–39 GLOBAL TRADE
WORLD TRADE ORGANIZATION
World Trade Organization <www.wto.org> Disputes
Gateway

THE BANANA DISPUTE
World Trade Organization <www.wto.org>

Food and Agriculture Organization <www.fao.org>
Commodities and Trade, Bananas

EXPORT SHARE
BananaLink <www.bananalink.org.uk>

BANANA EXPORTERS
FAO, Banana Notes <www.bananalink.org.uk/images/
stories/FAO%20BIN%202005.pdf

40–41 TRADE AND FOREIGN POLICY
IMPORTANCE OF TRADE
Calculation based on data provided by: TradeStats Express.
Presented by the Office of Trade and Industry Information
(OTII), Manufacturing and Services, International Trade
Administration, US Department of Commerce
<tse.export.gov>

SUBSIDIES: THE EXAMPLE OF COTTON
World Trade Organization <www.wto.org> Disputes
Gateway

WORLD COTTON EXPORTS
<www.nationmaster.com>, citing US Department of
Agriculture

US COTTON EXPORTS
TradeStats Express. Presented by the Office of Trade and
Industry Information (OTII), Manufacturing and Services,
International Trade Administration, US Department of
Commerce <tse.export.gov>

Chapter Three: CAPITAL

44–45 INVESTMENT
FOREIGN DIRECT INVESTMENT
US Department of Commerce: Bureau of Economic Analysis
<www.bea.gov>

46–47 MULTINATIONALS
US Department of Commerce Bureau of Economic Analysis
Press Release, April 20, 2006: William Zeile: *Summary
Estimates for Multinational Companies: Employment, Sales,
and Capital Expenditures for 2004*

IMPORTANCE OF MULTINATIONALS
RJ Mataloni, "US Multinational Companies: Operations in
2003," Bureau of Economic Analysis, July 2005, p17 <www.
bea.gov>

COCA-COLA EMPLOYEES
The Coca-Cola Annual Report 2006
<www.thecoca-colacompany.com>

48–49 CAPITAL TRANSACTIONS
NET FINANCIAL FLOW OF ASSETS
Department of Commerce: Bureau of Economic Analysis
<www.bea.gov> International Balance of Payments.
Downloaded December 2005

50–51 THE DOLLAR
DOLLAR EXCHANGE RATE
Trade Weighted Exchange Index: Major Currencies, Board of
Governors of the Federal Reserve System

DOLLAR DOMINANT
International Monetary Fund <www.imf.org> *Annual
Report 2005*

Chapter Four: PEOPLE

54–55 IMMIGRATION
IMMIGRATION; COUNTRY OF ORIGIN
REGION OF ORIGIN
US Department of Homeland Security, Immigration
Statistics <www.dhs.gov/ximgtn/statistics> *Yearbook of
Immigration Statistics 2005*, Tables 2 & 3

56–57 THE AMERICAS
HISPANIC POPULATION
MIGRATION FROM AMERICAS
US Department of Homeland Security, Immigration
Statistics <www.dhs.gov/ximgtn/statistics> *Yearbook of
Immigration Statistics 2005*, Table 3

INCREASE IN ILLEGALS; ILLEGALS
US Department of Homeland Security, Immigration
Statistics <www.dhs.gov/ximgtn/statistics> *Estimates of the
Unauthorized Immigrant Population living in the United
States: January 2005*

CUBAN MIGRANTS
US Department of Homeland Security, Immigration
Statistics <www.dhs.gov/ximgtn/statistics> *Yearbook of
Immigration Statistics 2004*

58–59 ECONOMIC MIGRATION
LARGEST MIGRANT POPULATIONS
FEMALE MIGRANTS TO THE USA
United Nations, *Trends in World Migrant Stock: The 2005
revision* <www.un.org/esa>

GLOBAL MIGRATION
LATIN AMERICAN REMITTANCES
Department of Economic and Social Affairs, UN: Population
Division, International Migration 2006 <www.un.org/esa>

FINANCIAL REMITTANCES
Inter-American Development Bank Multilateral Investment
Fund, *Remittances 2005 Promoting Financial Democracy*,
Washington DC, March 2006 <idbdocs.iadb.org>

60–61 POLITICAL REFUGEES
PEOPLE OF CONCERN
PEOPLE UNDER UNHCR MANDATE
United Nations High Commission for Refugees, 2005
Global Refugee Trends <www.unhcr.org>

Chapter Five: MILITARY

64–65 MILITARY SPENDING
US MILITARY SPENDING
Center for Strategic and Budgetary Assessments, based on
Department of Defense and Office of Management and
Budget Data

66–67 COMPARATIVE MILITARY SPENDING
MILITARY SPENDING PER PERSON
Nationmaster.com based on *CIA World Factbook*, 2005

MILITARY SPENDING AS % OF GDP
CIA World Factbook 2005

68–69 MILITARY AT HOME
HOME BASES
Department of Defense, *Base Structure Report, 2004*

TOTAL MILITARY SPENDING
MILITARY SPENDING PER PERSON
<www.census.gov/prod/2004pubs/03cffr.pdf>

70–71 MILITARY ABROAD
PEOPLE AND BASES
Defense Manpower Centre, Statistical Information Analysis Division
<siadapp.dior.whs.mil/personnel/MILITARY/history/hst0609.pdf>
Department of Defense: *Base Structure Report, 2004*

72–73 ARMS SALES
US ARMS SALES
SIPRI Yearbook, 2004 <www.sipri.org>

TOP TEN ARMS EXPORTERS
SIPRI Yearbook, 2005 <www.sipri.org>

Chapter Six: NATIONAL SECURITY

76–77 INTERVENTIONS: 1945–89
Zoltan Grossman <www.zmag.org/CrisesCurEvts/interventions.htm>
Global Policy Forum <www.globalpolicy.org/empire/history/interventions.htm>

78–79 INTERVENTIONS: 1990–2006
Zoltan Grossman <www.zmag.org/CrisesCurEvts/interventions.htm>
<academic.evergreen.edu/g/grossmaz/interventions.html>
Global Policy Forum <www.globalpolicy.org/empire/history/interventions.htm>

80–81 INTERVENTIONS: MILITARY AND COVERT
FORCES ABROAD
The Heritage Foundation
<www.heritage.org/Research/NationalSecurity/troopMarch2005.xls>

Chapter Seven: SOFT POWER

88–89 AID AND INFLUENCE
AID DONATED
OECD figures reprinted in *Global Issues*
<www.globalissues.org/TradeRelated/Debt/USAid.asp>

US OVERSEAS DEVELOPMENT AID
<www.oecd.org/dataoecd/42/30/1860571.gif>

US OVERSEAS MILITARY AID
US Department of State <www.state.gov/t/pm/ppa/sat/c14560.htm>

US FOOD AID
<www.fas.usda.gov/food-aid.asp>
<www.ewg.org/farm/progdetail.php?fips=00000&progcode=total>

90–91 RELATIONS WITH THE UN
UN FUNDING; CUMULATIVE ARREARS
Global Policy Forum
<www.globalpolicy.org/finance/index.htm>

Chapter Eight: IDEAS

98–99 HOW AMERICA SEES THE WORLD
PERCEIVED SECURITY THREATS; US FOREIGN POLICY GOALS; US VIEWS OF OTHERS
Chicago Council on Global Affairs, Global Views 2006, *The United States and the Rise of China and India: Results of a 2006 Multination Survey of Public Opinion*, 2006 <www.thechicagocouncil.org>

NATIONAL PRIDE
T.W. Smith & S. Kim, "National Pride in Comparative Perspective: 1995/96 and 2003/2004," *International Journal of Public Opinion Research*, 18 (Spring, 2006), 127–136.

100–01 HOW THE WORLD SEES AMERICA
OPINIONS ON THE USA
Pew Global Attitudes Survey, reports released June 23, 2005 and June 13, 2006
<pewglobal.org/reports/pdf/247.pdf>
<pewglobal.org/reports/pdf/252.pdf>

HOW THE WORLD CHARACTERIZES AMERICANS
Pew Global Attitudes Survey, report released June 23, 2005
pp25–26 <pewglobal.org/reports/pdf/247.pdf>

MIDDLE EASTERN ATTITUDES TO USA
Five Nation Survey of the Middle East Submitted to: Arab American Institute by Zogby International, December 2006
<aai.3cdn.net/96d8eeaec55ef4c217_m9m6b97wo.pdf >

104–05 CULTURE WARS
THE LANGUAGE OF THE WEB
<www.internetworldstats.com/stats7.htm>

Chapter Nine: THE FUTURE

108–09 THE WAR ON TERROR
KEY LOCATIONS IN THE WAR ON TERROR
Extraordinary rendition: Amnesty International
<web.amnesty.org/library/index/engpol300032006> and newspaper reports

CHANGING SUPPORT
Pew Global Attitudes Survey, report released June 13, 2006
<pewglobal.org/reports/pdf/252.pdf>

110–11 LEVELS OF RESISTANCE
SITES OF RESISTANCE
Stop the War Coalition <www.stopwar.org.uk/march20>
US Department of State <www.state.gov/s/ct/rls/fs/3/191.htm>

114–15 SUSTAINING THE EMPIRE
INCREASE IN OIL IMPORT DEPENDENCY
US DOE, EIA, *Monthly Energy Review*, May 2003, and *Annual Energy Outlook 2003* quoted by: Ian W.H. Parry and Joel Darmstadter, "The Costs of U.S. Oil Dependency" December 2003 • Discussion Paper 03–59, Resources for the Future, Washington DC]

THE BIG PLAYERS IN 2050
John Hawksworth, *The World in 2050: How big will the major emerging market economies get and how can the OECD compete?* PriceWaterhouseCoopers, March 2006

116–123 DATA TABLE
Population, Land area, GNI: World Development Indicators www.worldbank.org/data. Data for Cook Islands, Palestine Authority, Taiwan and Guam from *CIA Factbook*
Energy use and CO_2 emissions: Energy Information Administration, *International Energy Annual 2004*
Trade: TradeStats Express. Presented by the Office of Trade and Industry Information (OTII), Manufacturing and Services, International Trade Administration, US Department of Commerce.
Military spending per person: Nationmaster.com based on *CIA World Factbook*, July 28 2005
Arms imports from USA: Source: Sipri, 2004

PHOTO CREDITS